HEY GOD, DO YOU HAVE A MINUTE?

Learning to pray earnestly and

honestly.

Laurence C. Keene

Copyright

All rights reserved. No part of this book may be reproduced or transmitted in any form or by any means, electronic or mechanical, including photocopying, recording, or by an information storage and retrieval system - except by a reviewer who may quote brief passages in a review to be printed in a magazine or newspaper - without permission in writing from the author.

Printed in the United States of America

ISBN-13: 9780980023466
ISBN-13: 9780980023473

BISAC: Religion / Essays

Cover design by: Ernie Merlan

Recent books:

How Can I. . . ? Perplexing spiritual questions and suggestive spiritual answers

Hey God, Do You Have A Minute? Learning to pray honestly and earnestly

In production:

Searching for Home (an autobiography)

Dedicated To:

My five children: Lance, Kenneth, Bryan, Nancy, and Kathryn have been the source of so much of my joy in life. It is therefore, with considerable joy, I dedicate this book to them.

Table of Contents

Who Is the Real Person?	1
Tears That Help	3
A Newborn Baby!	5
Living A Dog's Life	7
The Silence Of Our Friends	9
Child Abuse	11
Abusing Pretty Faces	13
Showing Forgiveness	15
Warring With Bread	17
I Need Patience	19
Being Generous With My Praise	21
The Healing Power Of Kindness	23
Trusting What We Cannot Understand	25
Learning To Be Grateful	27
Being A Good Person	29
The Burden Of Imperfection	31
"He's a good man in the worst sense of the term."	33
Cultivating Good Manners	35
Touching Interesting Hands	37
Timely Thankfulness	39
Blessed Are The Givers	41
The Joy Of Playfulness	43

Wanting A Child's Eternity	45
Making A Good Impression	47
Read My Lips	49
Speaking And Listening	51
Seeing The Stars	53
Whose Face Is In The Mirror?	55
Thinking About Others	57
Learning To Trust	59
Giving With No Strings Attached	61
The Right Kind of Love	63
Struggling with Adversity	65
Navigating The Highs And Lows	67
The Loss Of Innocence	69
Healthy Self-Acceptance	71
The Terrible Feeling Of Loneliness	73
Grievances With Organized Religion	75
Warfare Among The Religious	77
Becoming Cynical	79
My Anger	81
Troubled Peacemakers	83
Moments Of Moodiness	85
Being Negative	87
A Good Night's Sleep	89
When I Am Discouraged	91
Alone In A Crowded Room	93

Coming From A Broken Home	95
A Penny For Your Thoughts	97
Finding Contentment	99
Being Glad To Be Alive	101
Our Wonderful World	103
Vacation Time	105
Being Carefree	107
A Successful Person	109
Happiness That Fits	111
God's Day Off	113
How A Good Memory Helps A Worrisome Heart	115
Making Things Perfectly Clear	117
When I Don't Know How To Pray	119
When I Don't Know What To Ask For	121
When I Am In A Hurry	123
Molehills And Mountains	125
Changing Times And Changing Perceptions	127
There Ought To Be A Law	129
Changing Along With Change	131
When I Am Envious	133
Good Taste	135
Sincerely Wrong	137
Forgetting Yourself	139
What A Saint	141
Angry Words	143

Savers And Non-Savers	145
Letting Go	147
The Bond Of Love	149
Cleanse Me	151
A True Friend	153
Grace Under Fire	155
Becoming Sensitive To A Grieving World	157
Becoming Satisfied With Less	159
Resting . . . One Day Of The Week	161
Shoes Tell The Story	163
Money Talks Eloquently	165
Creatures Of Habit	167
Older People	169
Time On My Hands	171
We Are All Unfinished Symphonies	173
Being A Father	175
Running Out Of Time	177
Feeling Young Again	179
Twenty Four Hours To Live	181
The Theft Of Childhood	183
The Divine Operator	185
Having An Easy Conversation	187
Heaven, The Answer For An Unfair World	189
God Is A Good Habit	191
I Believe In Miracles	193

Seeing Miracles	195
Miracles	197
Elevating The Obvious	199
God, Our Security	201
On My Knees	203
Angels On Earth	205
When To Look Up	207
Gaining My Senses	209
The Rat Race	211
Hurrying To Nowhere	213
Teenagers	215
Single People	217
Faking It	219
Making Excuses In Life	221
I Love Passionate People	223
In Between My First And Last Breath	225
Losing And Finding a Job	227
Have A Happy Birthday	229
The Fastest Way To Get Rich	231
When Someone Is Too Good To Be True	233
The Most Important Body Part	235
My Daughter Is Getting Married	237
Improving Our Prayer Aim	239
On Being Invited To Dinner	241
Hearing Clearly What Is Spoken	243

Making The Last Telephone Call	245
Laughter Is The Best Medicine	247
Praying To God In A Time of War	249
Leaving Well Enough Alone	251
Frightened To Death	253
True Greatness	255
Beautiful And Terrible Mornings	257
Putting Things Off	259
Surprised By Arrogance	261
Being In Charge Of our Feelings	263
A Laughing Matter	265
An Eager Learner	267
On Being A Failure	269
The Bed That Clarifies	271
The Bothersome Trail Behind	273
Moving God or Moving Me?	275
Some People I Like and Dislike	277
Growing Older	279
Compassion Or Justice?	281
Back-To-Back Religions	283
Humor	285
Things That Pleasure	287
Our Valentine Greetings	289
Healing Affection	291
My Grandchildren	293

Infinite Understanding	295
Ignorance And Arrogance	297
Talking But Not Listening	299
Religion And Politics	301
Crying Is Good Medicine Too	303
The Spoken Word	305
Tolerance And Intolerance	307
Enthusiasm	309
Angry Again?	311
Blessed Receiving	313
Supporting Falling Skies	315
Three Little Words	317
The Harmony Of Words And Heart	319
The Best Sentence	321
Shame And Guilt	323
Interest At First Sight	325
At The End	327
Thanks For the Memories	329
Fragrant Blessings	331
Down Time	333
Fixing People	335
Cynicism and Sarcasm	337
The Time Of Our life	339
Won't Power	341
From Something To Everything	343

Depressed And Sleepy	345
The Art Of Renunciation	347
Both Half Full And Half Empty	349
Hearing What I Didn't Say	351
Faith - A Decision	353
Living With Our Differences	355
Contented Eyes	357

Preface

I am not a person who is particularly attracted to prayers uttered in public places. I am often called upon to offer public prayers and I do so when I am asked to. However, the temptation to perform and pontificate in public places is very great. It is not easy to be honest and vulnerable in our public praying. One would think that it would be much easier to be honest with God in our private moments with him. But it isn't. Our need to try to impress the Almighty seems to know no boundaries.... even in private. The purpose of this devotional book of prayers is to help us talk to God in the way true friends try to speak to one another. True friends speak to one another about the full range of their human concerns and feelings without trying to either impress the other or be less than truthful in what they have to say. Praying to God should be our highest form of truth-telling. It is my hope that the prayers

I have chosen to share with you in this book will encourage the reader to be open and transparent before God and to speak the truth when he or she prays. You will notice that at the end of each prayer I do not conclude the prayer with the words: "In Jesus' name I pray, amen." I have chosen to do this purposely. I think every prayer we utter should be spoken in our own name, not someone else's. We should not think that invoking Jesus' name gives our prayer more power or makes it somehow more acceptable to God. I think it is the sincerity, the honesty, and the transparency of our heart before God that gives our prayer it's power and causes God to open his heart to our heart, not the speaking of some memorized phrase, as well-intentioned as it may be. An old Muslim leader once concluded his prayer with the words: "By the beard of Allah I speak these words." There are no beards in this book of prayers. My suggestion to you is that there should be none in yours as well.

Laurence C. Keene

Who Is the Real Person?

I walked into a large waiting room, dear God, and I saw the room filled with people I did not recognize. One person was merrily whistling an old tune I vaguely remember having once sung myself. He was filled with such joy I could hardly imagine why he was in this room. Everyone else seemed so different. The entire room was plagued with such a pall of gloominess that it seemed quite out of keeping with this man's happy demeanor. One man was eating a sandwich with his back to another for fear that the other person near him might ask for a bite. "If he thinks he's getting any of my sandwich he's got another think a comin'." I heard him mutter to himself. Two people were arguing over sitting rights to the softest chair in the room. Another person was cowered in the corner afraid that others might see the tears she was cleverly trying to hide with the magazine she had thrust in her face. One man was counting the money in his wallet for the tenth time and another man was looking at the knees of a woman whose skirt was far too short while she was standing and far too revealing when she sat down. "Who are these people?" I asked the attendant at the receptionist's desk. "Why, they are all **you,**" the attendant replied. "You have walked into the room of your inner self. These are the people you parade before all of us every day of your life. We see you very clearly. You seldom do. When the real you is asked to stand someday, I am afraid you will have to have a good-sized room to accommodate who you are." I left the room, dear God, and took all those pieces of me away.

Tears That Help

Dear God, I'm not usually at a loss for words but the other day the right words simply would not come to me. A dear friend had just related a personal tragedy to me. It broke my heart to hear her tell her story. The tears welled up in my eyes and I ached for her. I wanted to say something that would take her awful pain away but no perfect words would come out of my mouth. All of my training, all the books I had ever read, the many experiences I have had, none of them came to my defense, or more importantly, to her aid. I wanted the right words but only tears came. No words came. And then she said to me: "Thank you." And I said to her, "But I didn't say anything." She said, "Yes you did." Then she cried and a great peace came over her. I learned in that moment that it was not a time for saying. It was a time for doing. So, I did the most eloquent thing I knew how to do. I wept!

A Newborn Baby!

I saw a little baby girl born this morning, Lord. All of time was frozen for me. The earth stood still. The din of city life was silenced for the moment. There was only this one solitary voice in all the universe that captured my attention. Her first cry was as eloquent as the world's greatest orator. All who were in the birthing room wanted to touch her soft, pink skin. There was a sense of wonderment and awe and recognition that we were standing in the presence of one of God's wonderful miracles. Indeed, it was the miracle of creation itself. In that magical moment I learned that there are times, O God, when words fail to capture the beauty of a certain event. There are times when the beauty is not in the eye of the beholder. That infant's beauty would have been there even if that room had been empty or if everyone in that room had been blind. There are moments when even the heavens are silenced and poised to listen for certain sounds. The sound of a new-born baby's first cry is one of those moments. And when that happens, dear Lord, I can hear your loud, booming voice ring throughout the entire universe: "L' Chayim - to life!"

Living A Dog's Life

I have a new little puppy in my house, O Lord. It has been more than a half century since I have owned a dog. The years in-between had been too busy, it seemed to me, to have a dog. Academic degrees had to be earned. Children had to be raised. Jobs had to be worked at. My life had to be arranged and rearranged. It just seemed to me that life was too busy for a dog to be a part of it. But now that I have a dog again dear God, I cannot help but wonder if all that hard work wouldn't have gone a whole lot easier for me if I had owned a few puppies along the way. Every time I walk into my house that little puppy is deliriously happy to see me. Never once has she been upset with me, even in those times when I have momentarily ignored her. Dogs seem to be so willing to just wait for our irksome moods to pass and when they do they seem more than ready to give us all their stored-up love and affection when we are finally ready to give them even a little of our own. I have noticed that even so-called terrible people can have wonderful dogs. Dogs almost never seem to mirror their master's bad habits of intolerance, unkindness, and petty selfishness. In fact, dear Lord, we have a wonderful name for people who act like dogs. We call them saints. No matter how badly we treat these little furry ones they always return our meanness with generous amounts of affection and love. I sure am glad I have this loving puppy, dear Lord. I probably will never become a living saint but this little dog will certainly give me a better picture of what one is suppose to look and act like.

The Silence Of Our Friends

Dear God, it isn't what our enemies say about us that hurts us as deeply as what our friends do not say on our behalf. It is the silence of our friends, not the sound and fury of our enemies, that overwhelms us with the greatest feelings of sadness and aloneness. There have been moments in my life, dear Lord, when all I wanted to hear was a friend's voice speaking up on my behalf. A soft, even an inarticulate word of friendly support would have been enough to sustain my shaky feelings of self-confidence. In those moments of self-doubt I have not needed great oratory on my behalf. I just needed a word. A simple, supportive word would have been enough to quiet the opposing voices and revive my own shaken resolve in life. How bitterly barren I have felt when that voice has not been heard. I have felt silenced by my friends' silence. Help me, dear God, to speak up for my friends. Don't allow my friends to feel defeated by my lack of a timely response on their behalf. Help me to speak that supportive word on behalf of my friends, even as inarticulate as it might be. Help me to speak a word that will neutralize all the sounds of the universe that might rise against them. Help my one word of support to restore the courage and resolve of a friend to face down those demons that can often triumph over us when friends are silent.

Child Abuse

"Can I divorce my parents?" That is what the young girl said to me, Lord. She wanted to divorce her mother and father. Her parents had abused her in many terrible ways when she was a little child and they continued to do so to this very day. She felt that she was forever bound to them because they had given birth to her several years ago. Her parents thought that by giving birth to her they were permitted and entitled to continue in their abusive behavior toward her. This grieving, wounded girl didn't understand that her parents had already divorced her through their abusive conduct. Their parental contract had already been broken by their shameful behavior. The names 'mother' and 'father' were no longer appropriate names for them to wear. I told the young girl, dear God, that we often deserve the names we are given by others to wear. Names like: 'loafer,' 'freeloader,' 'addict,' and 'friend' are all earned names. I said to her that she didn't need to divorce and separate herself from her parents at all because they had already done that a long time ago. They had given up and discarded those good names they no longer deserved to wear. No child should ever have to divorce her parents, dear Lord. No parent should ever make them want to.

Abusing Pretty Faces

O Lord, I was talking with a person the other day who had a blemish on her face. It wasn't a very large blemish, in fact it was a very small one. However, I found myself focused on this one very small imperfection. She had a beautiful face but all I could see was this minor blemish. Her imperfection drew more of my attention than did the rest of her beautiful face. I went away thinking about that small, insignificant flaw in her appearance as if that flaw somehow defined who she was. I had missed the rest of her beauty because of my fixation on her blemish. It was almost as if her beauty didn't exist at all for me because I was so interested in seeing something else. I destroyed her beauty because of my own very narrow and critical perception of her. O God, why do we do this to one another? Why do we slay the beautiful and ignore the wonderful in the people we meet each day? What arrogance in us drives us to define the people we meet in the basest of terms instead of seeing your divine image reflected in each one of your children? Please, dear

Lord, give me a better eye to see the best in everyone I meet. The next time I find myself tempted to be critical of someone's face or character or appearance, please hand me a mirror.

Showing Forgiveness

Oh Lord, it is a wonderful feeling to feel forgiven by people we have wronged. There is no lower low in all of life than to have done something terribly wrong to another person and to feel as if that wrong will never be forgiven. We have all had that soul-numbing experience, dear Lord. We have walked around with a leaden heaviness in our heart wishing we could live previous foolish moments all over again or to prevent a terrible wrong we had done before from ever having occurred. How strong our need for forgiveness is, O God. And, oh when this forgiveness comes to us it is like a re-birth for us. It is like a resurrection; a reviving of our soul at the very door of death itself. Thank you, dear Lord, for placing in my pathway forgiving individuals. People who have the kindness to absorb my painful treatment of them with grace and who give me my life back again by forgiving me. So much like you these wonderful people are. They have given me not what I have deserved but what I have so badly needed. I am very grateful for what these dear forgiving people are teaching me and I am grateful, too. for what you have taught them.

Warring With Bread

I wonder what it would be like, dear God, to fight a war with bread. I know such a suggestion sounds nonsensical, but listen to me please, O God. For thousands of years we have been fighting our wars with increasingly sophisticated and devastatingly terrible new technologies. A long time ago we began warring with others by swinging huge clubs and throwing rocks at one another and today we launch terrible bombs and exploding rockets in each other's direction. When the warring is over, in every instance, it is never quite clear who is right, only who is left. And, whether the deaths are brought about by a rock or a rocket, dead is always dead. The winning dead and the losing dead are surgically removed from the pool of available human talent and resources that could have been used to construct a new and better world for everyone. What a waste, O God. Is there ever a good war? Is there ever a bad peace? Maybe we should fight with bread. Maybe we should try to kill our enemy with kindness. "How stupid," some would say. "How hopelessly naive," others might remark. "You don't deal with killers and tyrants that way," the wizened counselors among us would pontificate. Wait a minute, dear God. Who's being stupid and naïve? What is so smart and enlightened about trying warring methods that haven't worked since the beginning of time? How many more failed attempts at whoring after war do we have to endure before we learn that sticks and stones really do break our bones and that calling people names and making faces at our enemies really do bring about injuries that never quite heal. So, pass me some bread, dear God. Help me to shame my enemy with my kindness. Maybe he will choose to retaliate with a loaf of his own.

I Need Patience

Dear Father, I wonder if the saints of old would have had as much patience as they seemed to have had if they had to deal daily with such things as freeway on-ramps at five o'clock in the afternoon and ballpoint pens that never seem to write when we want to use them. It is so very difficult to remain patient in such an imperfect world as we live in today. If babies never cried in the middle of an important event and if the same people in life didn't seem to need our help dealing with the same problems over and over again, I think patience would be a virtue at which more of us would excel. My world must really be imperfect because there are a lot of imperfect people who really know how to push my buttons. I suppose my own lack of perfection disturbs their imperfect world as well. Is it possible that someone else is praying right now and asking for your help in having more patience with me? Please help me to be more patient with others so others won't have to pray so much and so often to have more patience with me.

Being Generous With My Praise

Dear God, we speak so many wonderful words about others at their funerals. Why is it that we tend not to speak these same wonderful words to one another daily when they can be heard and appreciated? I have witnessed the difference a timely word of praise can make in the life of a person who does not feel very worthwhile and who may doubt whether their contributions to life are of any real importance or significance to anyone. I have seen how people can come to life again as a result of one sincere and well-placed compliment given to them or a timely word of appreciation spoken for the smallest thing they might have done for someone else. Words! Life-giving, mood-enhancing words. How easy it is, dear God, for us to dispense these words lavishly. How easy it is for us to change the course of another person's miserable day. A simple word of praise from our lips is often enough to do it. A spoken compliment to a person who deserves one can turn the tide of someone's stormy day. A note of appreciation addressed to someone in the mail who went out of their way to do something helpful for another can restore the smile on a saddened face. So much better gifts are these expressions of praise than flowers given at a funeral or a spoken eulogy that will never be heard by the very person who needed to hear those life-giving words so much earlier.

The Healing Power Of Kindness

Kindness! What a wonderful moment it is, O God, when a kind person walks into our lives. We feel so very protected and encouraged when they walk into our space. So safe from the pain we often bring to ourselves and from the crushing harm that others sometimes inflict on us as well. There is such profound healing in a kindly spirit. The abrasions we often experience from being rubbed the wrong way in life are healed and soothed by the gentle voice or touch of a kind person. I am willing, O God, to overlook a multitude of imperfections in a person who just happens to also be very kind. I am not saying that I am in favor of those human frailties and faults these people may have but I am so much more in favor of the kindly nature they exhibit in spite of the many other imperfections they may possess. I am in favor of how, when everything else fails to restore my will to persevere in life, a kind response that comes my way will usually energize and motivate me to keep on keeping on. I know that everyone cannot be intelligent, witty, or gifted in the ways that usually make people sit up and take notice of them, but I know that we can all be more kind than we typically are. Help me to be a kind person, O Lord, even if no one stands up and immediately takes notice of my abilities or lack of them.

Trusting What We Cannot Understand

I am so full of questions, dear God. My need to have answers for all of my questions seems to know no bounds. I can understand why Adam and Eve were greatly tempted by the tree of the knowledge of good and evil in the Garden of Eden story in the Bible. The lust for perfect knowledge is certainly an old and powerful desire in most of us. It certainly afflicts me. Help me to understand more clearly, dear Lord, that being a happy and fulfilled person does not mean knowing all the answers to every question that may arise in my mind. I understand that possessing superior knowledge on any subject can easily create in us an arrogant spirit which sometimes accompanies this greater gift of knowing. Please curb my desire to think that I need to know all of the answers to all the questions in the universe. Help me to realize that arrogance is never an improvement on humility and that having a few friends left around me after most of my questions have been answered in life is also very important as well.

Learning To Be Grateful

Someone sent me a greeting card the other day, dear God, which had the two words "Thank you" written on it. What I had done for that person seemed so very insignificant to me. What that greeting card did for me, however, was very significant indeed. That person's expression of gratitude for me was so much greater than the small deed I felt I had done for him. Isn't that the way it always is with gratitude, O God? A thankful heart always turns the spotlight away from itself. A grateful heart always seeks to warm and nourish someone else's spirit. It seems to me, O Lord, that one person's gratitude is equally as important as another person's generosity. It often is more rare as well. There seems to be so much more generosity around these days than gratitude. I have heard people make the statement that "It is more blessed to give than to receive." I suppose it is, but isn't it also a blessed thing to receive graciously and gratefully as well, O God? I can't help but think that if we were all more grateful in our receiving that more people would behappier and more liberal in their giving.

Being A Good Person

I remember, O God, that Leo Durocher the famous big-league baseball manager once said: "Good guys finish last." I guess what he really meant was that if we want to get ahead in this life we must be very careful not to be one of the good guys. He seemed to be telling us that in order to be successful in life we should learn to be more treacherous, opportunistic, conniving and a whole lot of other things that would probably make an angel blush. I hope that isn't the case, O Lord. I don't want to think that the successful people in life are really nothing but wolves in sheep's clothing. I don't want to be convinced that the winners in life are only unseemly people hiding beneath a thin veneer of decency; bad people standing in the winner's circle of life dressed up in respectable clothing. I've seen some wonderful winners in life, O Lord; some really successful people who were also really good people. They were good and decent people all the way down to their underwear. They finished first in life but they didn't compromise their inner goodness in doing so. They didn't sell out or abandon their morality or their thorough-going goodness in their pursuit of their goals in life. I am grateful for these people I have known who have kept the angels from blushing. I am proud of them not because they finished first in life but, rather, because they finished with their honor and decency intact. Dear Lord, I don't think Leo knew everything he was talking about. He may have understood the physical power that makes a successful baseball player but he didn't seem to understand the spiritual and moral power within all of us that can produce a good and decent life. He didn't seem to understand, O God, that in the moral and ethical contests in life that bad people always finish last and that good people always come in first.

The Burden Of Imperfection

I wish I could do one single thing perfectly well so I wouldn't get so discouraged at the many things I do so imperfectly. I eat too much; I get angry too often; I think unkind and impure thoughts more than I would like to admit. I am also far too ambitious; too frequently I am jealous; and I am much less thoughtful than I know I ought to be. After decades of trying to improve myself one would think I would be getting more things right than I do. The truth is, I am not actually inventing a whole lot of new and foolish things to do each day. Instead, I find myself simply repeating the same old imperfect and destructive things I have done for a long time. I am having to re-learn those same old not-quite-learned lessons all over again. Practice has not made me more perfect. It has, instead, made me more discouraged and weary. Be patient with me, O Lord. Help me to be more patient with myself as well. If I act foolishly, please help me to make that foolish action a solitary occurrence. Keep me from the embarrassment and suffering of revisiting and repeating my old failed behaviors over and over again. I know that I am not yet what I ought to be. I just don't want to be stuck on what I once was.

"He's a good man in the worst sense of the term."

Dear Lord, I met a highly principled person the other day. He told me that his principles would not allow him to associate with certain kinds of people nor would they permit him to follow his friends into certain disrespectful places. He made it very clear to me that his principles came first to him even if other people were hurt or injured by his so-called principled decisions. But, O God, are principles more important than people? In the name of some exalted principle are we permitted to bring a sky-full of pain and injury down on others? If it comes to a choice between holding on to a principle or responding to someone's deep and important personal need, must we sacrifice the person in favor of the principle? God, something deep within me tells me that loving people is profoundly more important than loving principles. That loving people is the ultimate principle. Help me, O God, to keep this distinction clear in my mind. I think I would rather be guilty of being a little less principled in life than being a whole lot less loving and caring as I move on through my somewhat principled life.

Cultivating Good Manners

"Have a nice day!" "Excuse me, please." "Thank you, sir." It is wonderful, Lord, to hear and to receive such gracious gestures of civilized speech. These are words, however, that seem increasingly to be the forgotten gestures from another time and place. How wonderfully pleasant these civilized words are to hear, dear God. They lubricate the sometimes abrasive daily connections we have with one another. They help to manage the hectic traffic of our human wills as we try to move in and out of one another's lives. They provide the respect that is so vital in risking the openness and trust we want to have with others. Dear God, help me to be more polite and courteous toward others. Keep me aware of how deeply wounded others can sometimes feel when they are treated without civility. I know it is not easy to always have the best manners or to use the right gestures that are needed for the difficult moments in our lives. Help me to find the most civil and gracious way to encounter the people I meet each day. Please don't let any rudeness or brutishness on my part diminish another person's experience with me today. Oh, and by the way, thank you very much for listening to me.

Touching Interesting Hands

Dear Lord, I held some interesting hands today. I held the hand of an elderly lady who whispered in my ear her fearful awareness that she was quickly coming to the end of her life. I held the hand of a young man afflicted with the AIDs virus and of a young woman who was told by her doctor that she had cancer. Both of these very courageous people were trying to find the strength to be brave and hopeful in the very face of diseases that often strip people of much of the confidence and sometimes even the willingness to persevere in life. I held the hand of a young bride-to-be who could hardly sit still because of the penned-up excitement of her coming wedding day. And then, best of all, I held the hands of a little baby. Soft, un-calloused, trusting, and firmly grasping little hands. So unlike the well-worn hands that usually grip my own each day. I could not help but think what these different hands had given me this day, dear God. Each one, in their touching me, had left me more connected at the end of the day to the wonderful fullness of life around me than I had felt earlier in the morning. I finished the day with more understanding, with more courage, with more excitement for my next day, and with more trust in the goodness of others than I had when my day had begun. All of this came to me because of the touch of someone else's hands. Thank you for my hands, dear God. I think that somehow people's hands must be connected to their hearts in some important way because every time I found myself reaching out and touching some other person's hands I also felt their hearts as well. I certainly hope, dear Lord, as I end this day that the other peoples' hearts I felt touched by today were richer too for having touched my hands as well.

Timely Thankfulness

Dear God, I remember when my grandmother bought me an expensive book for my high school graduation gift. She spent her entire month's small pension salary for that book. It was a copy of the Holy Bible. I was a busy teenager at the time who was going to thank her some day in the future when I could find the time. Sadly, my grandmother found the time to die before I found the time to be grateful. I learned an important lesson that day, O Lord. I learned that thanking someone quickly for the good they have done is so much better than thanking them slowly for it. I have also learned that when I am late in thanking someone for their kindness or generosity that it gets easier and easier to simply not thank them at all. Once a certain amount of time passes it is almost impossible to thank someone without our insincerity nullifying or weakening the very words of gratitude we eventually try to speak. When I have waited too long to express my gratitude for a kindness that someone has extended to me, my avoidance of the other person is often the foolish alternative I begin to follow. Avoidance becomes my cowardly way of choosing to save my face at the terrible expense of my losing a generous friend. God, keep me grateful. Give me the timely words with which to express my gratitude. I would so much rather have an on-going closeness with a generous friend than an ungrateful feeling in my heart that has to resort to peeking around every corner in my life to avoid meeting up with the people who have done nothing wrong in life except to be kind and generous to me.

Blessed Are The Givers

Dear Lord, someone once said: "It is more blessed to give than to lend, and it costs about the same!" I think that a big part of the joy of birthdays and anniversaries is the thrill of giving presents or gifts and then watching the growing expressions of excitement on the faces of those receiving them. I think that it would be impossible, O God, to create such a feeling of happiness and joy by simply loaning gifts to people on these very special occasions. How silly it would be to do such a thing. It is true that a lot of people are earning a great deal of money these days making loans to people but I don't think there is very much joy in doing that. I think we all should be cheerful givers. The simple truth is that most of us actually feel so much more cheerful when we are giving, not taking. Help me to be a generous giver, dear God, not a taker. Help me to give enough to make someone else happy and then help me to give even a little more until it finally makes me happy.

The Joy Of Playfulness

I was watching the little children stepping on their shadows the other day, dear Lord. They were actually trying to run after their little child-like shadows. Their game went on and on for several minutes. They were lost in their playfulness. I looked at their faces and I saw my face reflected in one of them. But all of a sudden my face vanished and it wasn't my face at all. My vision of my own childhood passed away as quickly as it came. My own playful spirit vanished too. Just a vapor for a moment extinguished by adult realities. I miss that little child in me. I miss those playful moments when the most serious thought I had was to successfully step on my own shadow. I think I understand why adults look so longingly at children who are busy playing and why children absolutely never look the same way at adults who are busy working. I think children understand something the rest of us adults have forgotten. Please, dear God, revive some of the child in me so I can remember and more fully understand what a magnificent gift I once had and, hopefully, can find and enjoy again.

Wanting A Child's Eternity

I saw a little child the other day Lord. I mean I looked intently at him. This was no mere glance-in-his-direction kind of look. It was a long and thoughtful look on my part. The child was humming an unrecognizable tune. A moment later he was caressing an old worn stick with his stubby little fingers. There was no worry or stress on his face, only the complete absorption in that moment's discovery of a worn stick that would not have captured any adult's attention. Time seemed to stand still for this little child. Past, present, and future all seemed to be compressed between his little fingers. Eternity was in his hands. O Lord, I want to find that stick and hum that tune again. I want the kind of face that little child possessed.

Making A Good Impression

Dear God, I heard a mother say to her little child the other day: "Be careful what you say. I want you to make a good impression." That is what most of us are busy trying to do each day, dear God. We are trying to make good impressions. We are trying to be so very careful with what we do before others because if we are not very careful we feel that our impressions may not always be very attractive ones. Maybe that is our problem. Maybe we are just simply trying too hard. Maybe we impress the least when we try to impress the most. Maybe the more careful we are at getting our impressions right the more often we end up getting them all wrong. Please help me, Lord, to present myself as I am and not as I think someone else wants me to be. Keep me from dressing up my true self in false appearances that no one who truly knows me would ever recognize as being the real me. Whatever I am on any given day, let it be honestly me and not some close approximation of the real thing. Help me to love myself as I truly am so I can put everyone at ease who meets me knowing they have met the 'real thing.' Make a good impression on me, dear God, so I won't have to be so concerned with making one on everyone else.

Read My Lips

I was talking to you, O Lord, in a public place the other day. My words were so softly spoken I could barely hear the words myself. My lips were visibly moving to express some urgent feeling I wanted to share with you when a woman interrupted my soliloquy and said to me: "Pardon me, were you speaking to me?" "No," I said, "I was just speaking to myself." I wasn't really just speaking to myself, O God, I was also speaking to you as well. But I didn't say those words to that lady. I don't know why I didn't tell her the full truth. She certainly looked like a nice enough person. I think I was just a little embarrassed to do so. I was caught off guard with the spiritual side of me exposed. In this two-dimensional, materialistic world we live in I was quickly brought down to earth by her question. I felt uncomfortable. I felt as though she wouldn't have understood where I was in that special moment of my spiritual reverie. I also think I felt a little disturbed toward her to have been removed from the sacred place I had been previously lifted to in my mind. I know

I did not wish to return very soon to a place of such ordinariness in my thoughts. I suppose I should have told her the truth. Maybe my truth would have lifted her to a better place as well. Help me, dear Lord, to keep speaking to you in public places. Help me to have the courage to simply let others read my lips and help me to not be so bothered by other people's wondering about my private wanderings.

Speaking And Listening

Generally speaking, Lord, I think women talk more than men. It seems to me that in everyday social interaction that women tend to talk more to others and men tend to listen more to them. I am not making any judgment about this interesting difference between men and women but I can see where this inclination and practice on the part of both men and women could become a source of real frustration between them. I can imagine a woman wishing that her male friend or partner would open up and talk more to her and I can imagine her male friend or partner wishing that his female friend or partner would simply talk less and listen more to his words, some of them sometimes spoken in muted periods of silence. It is not an easy thing, O Lord, to always know when to speak and when not to. I am sure you have that problem with all of us from time to time. I suppose there are times when you wish we would just keep quiet and listen to your voice and other times, of course, when your heart aches for us to open up and speak our truthful words to you. I am able to speak and I am able to listen, dear God, but I am not always very good at knowing when to open my mouth and speak and when to open my ears and just listen. Help me to have a better sense of timing. I certainly don't want to be guilty of keeping my mouth shut when the right word could make some difficult situation better. Nor do I want to be guilty of covering an important quiet listening moment with unimportant babbling on my part that could keep me from hearing what I should have heard in the first place.

Seeing The Stars

Dear God, I have noticed from a lifetime of observing people, that there are two distinctly different kinds of individuals I encounter on a daily basis: those who look upon their circumstances in life and see nothing but mud, and others who look around themselves and only see stars. Mud and stars. They are both there, to be sure, but most of us tend to be either the one kind of person or the other. I saw a woman the other day standing knee-deep in mud but all she could see around her were stars. I have seen others standing on the crest of a high mountain on a crystal clear night and all they could see around them was mud. What many wonderful people see in life, O Lord, doesn't seem to depend on where they are positioned in life at all. Their viewpoint doesn't always depend upon their viewing point. It depends on the kind of person they are in the first place. Help me, dear Lord, that when I am up to my knees in discouragement that you enable me to see a few stars even in the midst of such muddy circumstances. I am not asking for you to change the specific places where my feet are currently planted. I am not asking for you to get rid of the mud that sometimes engulfs me. I am just asking that you help me to change the way I look at the dismay that once in a while comes my way. Keep me from seeing less in life when I could be so much more blessed by seeing more. Don't let the mud in my life keep the stars from shining for me.

Whose Face Is In The Mirror?

"I'm trying to find out who I am!" That's what she said to me, Lord. She was 40 years old at the time she spoke those words to me and she still didn't have the answer to her quest. She didn't know who she was last year either or the year before that. She had been looking for that answer for a very long time. I couldn't help but think to myself, dear God, that perhaps that was exactly who she really was all along: she was a person perpetually trying to find herself. A person profoundly focused on herself I might add. She seemed to be a self, seeking a self. A person in a house of mirrors seeing only herself no matter in what direction she looked. Is it possible, dear Lord, that her problem was not that it was her self which was alluding her at all but rather that she was far too intoxicated and preoccupied with her self to ever find it? That in perpetually seeking who she was that she was only indulging herself, kidding herself, and ultimately losing herself in herself? Lord, I am struck by the thought that the great religious leaders in history never made statements like this young lady did. They were never trying to find out who they were at all. They were trying to find out who you were, O God or how they could find some greater truth than themself. Help me, O Lord, in my search for greater spiritual understanding. Help me to realize that there is only one important face in my house of mirrors. Keep me from thinking that it is mine.

Thinking About Others

"It was her thinking of others that made you think of her." That is what someone once wrote of Elizabeth Barrett Browning, dear God. I think all of us would want someone to say something like that about us. I wish I were more thoughtful in that way. I keep thinking that if I just had more time available to me each day I would be more thoughtful of others. Somehow I know in my heart that this is simply not true. I know that thoughtfulness is not a matter of having extra time. I am convinced that thoughtful people really don't have more free time than anyone else. They just have more heart. They have more concern. They have more compassion. I know my problem, O Lord. I spend so much time thinking about myself each day that I have so little time left at the end of it to think about anyone else. I do think good thoughts about others once in awhile, dear Lord, but help me to be more generous in outwardly expressing them when and where they will do the most good. I certainly don't want someone to say about me someday: "It was his thinking of himself that made me want to ignore and forget him!"

Learning To Trust

Dear God, it is not always an easy thing to trust people. It is not easy particularly if our trust has been broken or betrayed at an earlier time in our life. There are times when I think that there is no pain quite like the pain of a trust that has been violated. But upon more careful reflection I think there is a pain that is even greater than that. I think perhaps the pain of living a life where we would never want to trust anyone again would be an even greater pain than the pain of a trust that had previously been broken. The pain of not wanting to trust again would prevent any closeness with another person again. This unwillingness to trust others would destroy our care-free, unguarded existence with potential friends or lovers. We would, in effect, be building a fortress around our feelings and placing a lock on our heart. What a terrible price to pay for pain-prevention in life. And after all of those careful precautions on our part to keep from getting hurt again we would be left with the greatest pain of all: our aloneness. Please help me to do once again those many little things I once did in order to create the ability to have trust in others. Help me to know that just because I once unfortunately lost the treasure of someone else's closeness that this wonderful treasure can actually be found and enjoyed once more. Help me to understand that the pain of living with not ever being able to trust another person would be a far greater pain than the pain of living without the life-sustaining closeness that trusting another person can truly bring. O God, it seems to me that having what can possibly be lost is always superior to losing what can never be had again.

Giving With No Strings Attached

Dear God, I went to visit some people in jail the other evening. I looked around the room during the hour of visitation and I noticed a genuine outpouring of love from the other visitors toward those inmates. I wondered to myself if any of these inmates would have visited me if our positions were reversed. As quickly as I had that thought in my mind it occurred to me that it doesn't really matter whether any of these inmates would or would not have visited me. The truth is that love and compassion for others has to be given away not merely traded for someone else's promise of a return favor. Help me to remember, O God, that if my love for others isn't given freely that it really isn't love at all that I am giving away. Rather, I am merely engaging in bartering. Help me to love and freely give of my heart to others with no strings attached. Keep me from making deals with my generosity. Guide me away from calculating thoughts of how my efforts might benefit me. I hope I never have to spend any time in jail. However, if I do, I hope there are people around who are willing to visit me and to care for me without keeping score in their generous attempts at showing me their heart and loving compassion.

The Right Kind of Love

Lord, I have been recently talking to some people about the subject of love and what they thought love meant to them. Some of these people were very lonely and had been searching for a long time for a close and loving relationship with someone special. None of them had seemed to have found the right person with whom to share their love. Other people I have spoken to, however, have managed to experience the exciting fulfillment that rediscovered love can bring only to have that love somehow mysteriously slip away from them and then were left once again with that profound sadness which is so similar to what is felt when a death occurs. Still others have told me of living for years with a love partner only to find their love gradually reduced to routine obligations performed in ritualized ways with little of the original excitement and none of the soul-stirring satisfaction it once had when love was first born within them. Dear God, help us all to love better. Help us to keep alive that persistent and energizing force within us that we once enjoyed. Fill us more fully with your kind of persistent and soul-enriching love so that we can be more successful in maintaining our own as well.

Struggling with Adversity

She was so young and she was blind. She couldn't bear the darkness that enveloped her every waking day. In a moment when the weight of that darkness was too much for her to carry any longer, she took her life. Twenty four years of light-less life were over for her. God, that could have been me. I could have been that blind child. I could have been the infant born with some crippling disease. I could have been the polio victim or the hemophiliac. I could have been the bearer of the AIDs virus received from a blood transfusion. How fortunate I have been in so many ways. I have been so greatly blessed in life but more often than not I am quite unaware of that profound and glorious fact. How great is our need for a fuller expression of gratitude, O Lord. We breathe the air of many priceless political freedoms. We enjoy a standard of living that is the envy of the entire world. We push buttons and pull levers that make our daily work-tasks easier. We live like kings on commoners' salaries. O God, we are so blessed. Wash our repetitious complaints out of our mouths. We don't have to look very far to see other people around us who are trying to survive with very few resources to help them. These heroic people struggle mightily to carry burdens that would buckle our knees if we were called upon to carry them. Help me to be more helpful to those around me who are struggling and possibly running out of their light. And more importantly, dear God, maybe some of them are actually running out of their time as well!

Navigating The Highs And Lows

Dear God, I was thinking this morning of the words of an old spiritual I used to sing when I was a young boy. The words went like this: "Sometimes I'm up. Sometimes I'm down! Sometimes I'm almost to the ground." I often feel that way. Sometimes I feel as if I am grounded in some bad way. I feel afraid, or worried, or discouraged, or unmotivated. A soul trying to move ahead without much energy or a soul feeling just plain flat. But there are other times, to be sure, when I feel like a soul who is way up high flying with the eagles. I don't want to continue to be that kind of person, dear God, who sometimes feels up and sometimes feels down. I want to be more predictable and steady in my daily sojourn. I don't want to feel like I have to sometimes paint a contented face on a discontented spirit. Give me a jubilant spirit that abides; the kind of spirit that is the same in one season and the same in the next season as well. I don't want to be like the ocean tides that move nowhere but only repeat their highs and lows year after year after year. Make me more like a steady, flowing stream whose gentle path cuts a predictable course from a definite beginning to a definite end. Give me a steady and predictably glad heart so I can navigate more successfully through my world. Keep me from making my world more difficult than it has to be in my desire to move happily through it. And, finally dear Lord, create a receptive and patient heart within me to wait for those uplifting and rewarding feelings that I know will inevitably come my way for doing these good things which will help lift my walking feet to land at least six inches off the ground along my way! Not too high up or too low down but, somehow, just right for me to feel more like a moving river in life that is truly going somewhere in life not just like a moving tide beaching on the very same sand over and over again leaving me with a soul-numbing feeling that I have already been here and done that before!

The Loss Of Innocence

I saw a little child lose something the other day, dear God, which troubled me greatly. I saw him lose his innocence. It is a very sad thing to see someone lose their innocence. It seems that once our innocence is lost the whole world begins to look differently to us. Nothing appears the same anymore. The innocence we enjoy as children so affects our perception of the people and things around us. So does our loss of it. Do we have to lose our innocence, dear God, before we can see and understand the full truth of the world we live in? Is this child-like innocence only a temporary protection against seeing things as they really are until we are finally able and ready to see the full and complete truth of things? I want to see my world as it truly is, dear God. I don't want the truth around me to be distorted or misrepresented to me, but is this loss of our child-like innocence the price we have to pay for grown-up eyes? I was so saddened when I saw that little child lose his innocence the other day. Was this necessary loss the only way this child could ever become truly wise and ready for this grown-up world?

Healthy Self-Acceptance

She was filled with shame, dear Lord. She was filled with guilt too. She had not lived up to the expectations other people had of her and shame was what she felt because of her failure to do so. But the shame she felt was not nearly as great a burden for her to carry as was the guilt she carried within her as well. The guilt was there because she had not lived up to her own expectations either. Her guilt was a much heavier burden than was her shame. She could hardly move forward with her life, dear God. These twin encumbrances of shame and guilt had slowed her life to a crawl. She had no ambition. She had no joy. She had little hope for anything better in life. She was overwhelmed by the twin burdens of not measuring up to what others wanted her to be and not living up to her own expectations either. It seems to me, O Lord, that there is nothing heavier to carry in the whole wide world than the burden of a life we are not proud of. Please help us in those burdensome moments when we feel overwhelmed with exaggerated feelings of guilt and shame which rob us of so many of our future possibilities. Guide us to find a healthy self-acceptance that will not only restore the light-hearted feelings we once enjoyed but will also renew our joy and zest for life once more. Keep us from taking our future hostage by being too severe in the way we evaluate the failings of our past.

The Terrible Feeling Of Loneliness

My house seems so empty, dear Lord. My life's partner has been away for a few days and there are no sounds in the house except my own. How empty a house can be when there are no sounds in it except one's own. I have been thinking lately of the many people I know whose husband or wife or partner has died and the surviving partner has been left alone in a soundless, empty house. An empty house that will not soon be filled again with the sounds of a give-and-take relationship. Empty houses that no longer seem quite so full or complete when only one person is left to occupy them. How empty a kitchen table can be, dear Lord, when there is no one present to sit and eat on the other side of it. How much less melodious a song is when there is no one else nearby to hum along with. How much less funny a humorous story is when there is no other person's laughter to mingle with one's own. Be with us lonely people, dear Lord. Sit across the table from us and eat with us. Hum with us. Laugh with us. We need to hear some sounds other than our own. Make some noise, dear God. We need to know and feel that we are not alone in all this living business.

Grievances With Organized Religion

She sat, dejected, in my office, dear God. Her comments to me centered around the fact that she was planning on quitting the religious organization she had attended since her childhood and that she felt she needed to tell someone about her decision. I asked her why she had given up on organized religion. Her response was not brief. She had come to my office with a long list of grievances which she poured out to me as if she had been practicing her speech for a long while. She told me that organized religion, as she had experienced it, was intolerant and judgmental and that it often discriminated against women and other minorities. She pointed out that many of the religious groups she knew claimed to believe in certain cherished truths that all other religious groups were blind to. She spoke about her experiences with religious leaders who were overwhelmingly self-righteous and more eager to remove the speck from other people's eyes than they were to remove the huge log from their own eyes. She talked about religious organizations being as materialistic as the rest of society. She talked about them spending much of their money erecting physical monuments to their own egos while the hungry and needy in their midst were largely left ignored. O God, what a terrible impression organized religion sometimes creates in the minds of earnest seekers of truth. This woman seemed to be a caring person. I could have argued with her I suppose, but I did not do so. I felt I needed to listen to what she had to say. I needed to be reminded that it is very easy to get off track and to lose our way even when we are trying to do good things for others in an 'organized' religious way. I have been told that the truth sometimes hurts. Perhaps that explains why there was such considerable pain left in my office after she walked out the door.

Warfare Among The Religious

O God, it is sometimes very difficult to get along with religious people. I mean it is sometimes difficult to get along with people who claim to be followers of the Almighty. It never ceases to amaze me how people who claim to be speaking for you, O God, can be filled with such belligerence and animosity toward one another. That thought frightens me. It is almost as if your children see each other as being the enemy. It sometimes feels as if there is a war going on down here. Not a cosmic battle between the forces of good and the forces of evil, but rather a war between the true believers, those so-called good people, themselves. It is not a pretty sight. Their words are often very harsh. The spirit they express towards one another is sometimes exceedingly mean. Cruel judgments and spiteful recriminations are commonplace reactions they often have toward one another. Sometimes even very devout people are hurtfully demeaned by these purveyors of so-called religious truth. I think the Devil must chuckle when he sees this happen among us. Hell must be full of glee. But, I don't feel very much like laughing. Too many so-called good people are killing one another with unkindness these days. My grandmother used to tell me to kill people with kindness. I like my grandmother's way the best.

Becoming Cynical

Lord, she had such nice things to say about me, my wife, and my family. She was dressed rather poorly and I was waiting for her to ask me once again for money. She had asked me for money many times before. I had always given her financial help each time she had asked me and I was committed to keep helping her in this way. Here she was again, Lord, coming to me and asking me for money one more time. "I won't make this a habit," she said to me. Asking for money from others had become a habitual way of life with her. Her verbal litany was the same four years ago when I met her and gave her money for the first time. There doesn't seem to be much originality in the language of poverty dear Lord so keep me from becoming cynical when I encounter the poor over and over again with their repetitious and inarticulate entreaties for financial assistance. I want to be wise in my generosity toward others but I don't want to become calloused or cynical toward them in the process. It isn't easy to continue to have a soft heart when other people's hard times last for years and years. How can I know when I am really being helpful through my generosity toward others and when I am simply contributing to their delinquency. I think I need your helping hand in this. I'll try not to make my continual asking for help from you to become a habit on my part.

My Anger

Dear God, there are some emotions I experience which trouble me. One of them is my anger. There are times in my life when I suppose I should get angry. I know I should get angry when little children are abused and when justice is lacking in our response to calloused wrongdoing around us. I know I should get angry when mercy is denied to a truly penitent offender. I am fully aware that I should get angry at willful and shameful violations of high and noble obligations and standards. But most of the time my anger is usually not so noble. Mostly my anger is my arrogant response to someone else's view of things which I feel is less right than my own. My anger is most often the expression of my frustration at not being allowed to have my own selfish way about things. My anger is usually more self-righteous than righteous. When I think seriously about it I am embarrassed and ashamed of my anger. Please help me, dear God, from getting so worked up about the things in life that really do not matter very much. Calm me down so I can have some energy left over for the things that really do matter. Help me to find some nobility about the things that upset and anger me.

Troubled Peacemakers

The students at our local high school rioted today, Lord. They threw bottles, cans, and rocks at each other and shouted derisive names at one another as well. A few days later a young girl was driving her car home from the religious services she was attending and was shot to death in broad daylight. Today a young man was killed by a gunman as he was shopping at the local grocery store. There is so much pain and insanity in our world these days, O Lord. Something very evil has gotten hold of our thinking. Keep us safe from such harm, O God. Protect the people who nurture decency and who try to express kindness in the things they do each day. Give us the courage and strength we need to not give in to the prevailing cynicism and ugliness that blankets so many among us with a rage and hatred that diminishes and destroys the beautiful world around us piece by piece and person by person. Help us to develop the wisdom and desire to become peacemakers in a world that seems to be making less room each day for such healing gestures.

Moments Of Moodiness

I have a bad cold this morning, God. I feel terrible and I don't feel like doing very much. I know I should have more to say to you right now but I don't have the energy or the desire to talk to anyone today, even to you. There are a lot of people around me, I suppose, who are sick as well. I wonder if they feel very much like talking either. Why are there so many moments when we have so much to say to you and other moments when we don't have anything to say at all? Our moods seem to change from one moment to the next and yet you patiently endure our emotional highs and lows. You continue to listen to us on our good days and our bad ones. I wish I could be more consistent with my attention and interest in spiritual conversations. I am very grateful for the fact that you are steadfast in your willingness to listen to me even when I'm not very good company. Thank you for your attentive ear when I am willing to talk and for your patient ways when I am not.

Being Negative

Dear God, I spent a great deal of time the other day with a very cynical person. It had been such a long time since I had been exposed to such overwhelming negativity. When my day with him was over I felt completely drained of my energy and hopefulness. It was as if my inner light had been turned off and I was left with only my darkness. The birds stopped singing for me. No one was heard whistling a happy tune. The world seemed tilted to one side and I felt tilted along with it. How cruel life must have been to this person to have led him to look at life in such a mean-spirited and cynical way. What made his dark experience so terrible for me was that his attitude not only robbed the light and music from his own soul but it robbed some of the light and music from mine as well. It was so sad that his joyous spirit had been silenced. But it was just as sad that he had succeeded in silencing, for the moment, the chorus of joy within me at the same time. A couple of days have passed since then, O Lord, and the light inside me has come back on again. The birds are singing once more. My hope is up and running again and I am whistling a happier tune. It was a good reminder to me, O God, of just how terrible darkness can be and how easy it can be to get lost in it. Thank you for providing that wonderful life-giving light again for me. Thank you, too, for the birds and their sweet music.

A Good Night's Sleep

A man said to me the other day, Lord: "I wish I could go to sleep and never wake up again." My first impression was that this man must have wanted to die. Upon clearer reflection I realized that what he really wanted to do was to live. He had become so burdened with the problems and decisions that had to be made by him each day that he was totally overwhelmed by life. His cry was a cry for relief. Relief from the daily pressures of too many issues to have to deal with. Too many problems to solve. Too many crises to overcome. The quality of his life had become seriously eroded and he wanted his old more tranquil life back again. He wanted that former life that enabled him to sleep restfully at night. The kind of life where he could look forward to waking up in the morning. Not the kind of life where the additional sleep each night was only a partial remedy for his overwhelming daily demands. Dear God, help me to eliminate the things in my life which crowd out joyous living. Keep me from the seductive temptation to rush to nowhere. Help me to not bankrupt my future peace by carelessly overspending the precious, limited moments you give me each day. Keep me from overloading my life with things that can either be put off or put away for another time. Help me to want to wake up in the morning as badly as I wanted to go to sleep the previous night.

When I Am Discouraged

Discouragement! If there is anything that resembles a flat tire in the whole range of human emotions, dear God, it is discouragement. When I am discouraged it is as if all of my confidence and self-assurance have been badly punctured and I am left to slowly and painfully roll along through life as if I was moving along on flat tires. And, as I roll along on my miserable rims I feel every painful bump and imperfection along my way. There is nothing as discouraging as discouragement. It feeds on itself. Discouragement looks sadly at its own downcast face and reproduces its gloom and unhappiness on every reflective surface it finds. Discouragement sees no warming sunlight in a newly-painted room. It smells no freshly-baked bread in a mother's enticing kitchen. It does not feel or respond to a child's playful invitation to run, walk, or simply to sit alone together for a blissfully shared moment. Discouragement effectively shuts down the very best part of us, O God. It turns the light out inside us and we are left to move along pretending that no one is at home within us. No one to hurt and no one to grieve. But the simple truth is, Lord, I am hurting and I am grieving, Lord. Help me to put the courage back into my discouragement. Help me to find the faith that can put my courage where it can do the most good. I understand the wonderful difference a little bit of courage can make in life. When that courage is missing within me I know the difference its loss can make as well. I want to smell the bread again. I want to play with that little child again. I need those blissful moments to return to me.

Alone In A Crowded Room

There were many people in that crowded room, dear Lord, but I felt all alone within it. People were exchanging warm and intimate greetings with one another but no one greeted me. It was as if I was invisible. I was the new face in the room. Friends were seeking out old friends. They looked past me and embraced one another with their laughter and their warmth, but no one embraced or laughed with me. What a terrible affliction loneliness can be. Being lonely in a crowded room is the ultimate paralysis. There is no easy movement away from it, dear God. Once uncaring people make us invisible by their lack of interest or concern for the stranger in their midst, the paralysis of loneliness numbs and weakens all our responses. We are left with the overwhelming sense of the insignificance that belongs to invisible things. It is more than merely feeling small. It is the profound sense of being non-existent. Not there. Not important. Please, dear God, keep me from erasing someone by my lack of awareness of their presence in my life. Give me a clearer vision to see the lonely people in a room instead of looking past them to see someone or something else that is more familiar to me. Open my eyes so I can be more aware of the invisible, paralyzed people in every room that no one else knows is there.

Coming From A Broken Home

Dear Lord, I heard someone the other day speak about a certain child as coming from a broken home. I knew what that person meant. He meant the child's parents were divorced or separated from each other and that the child was living in a home with only half the number of parents he or she should ideally have. But, O God, this child's home didn't really seem broken at all to me. Both of his parents were wonderfully loving parents. Both parents deeply loved this child, even though their original love for each other no longer existed. This child's home was working. In fact, it was working quite well. It was a loving, caring, happy place. It wasn't broken. It seems to me, Lord, that homes aren't really broken by simply reducing the number of parents who are present in the home. We don't speak of a home where one of the parents has died as a broken home. Isn't it true, dear God, that homes are only broken when they fail to do what homes are supposed to do? They are broken when parents, for one reason or the other, do not provide the love and nurturing or the feelings of serenity, safety, guidance and encouragement that homes are supposed to provide for the young. I have seen homes where both parents are present that are broken in this way. These are homes that aren't working at all in caring for the young they have produced. Help us, dear God, to mend our homes and also to mend the language we use in talking about them. Help us to understand that not every home that looks broken really is, and that not every home which looks perfect is beyond the need of being fixed and made a bit better.

A Penny For Your Thoughts

"A penny for your thoughts." is what my old friend once said to me, Lord. I knew what she said had nothing to do with money at all. It had to do with intimacy. She wanted to know my thoughts. She wanted to know my feelings and longings. But, for the moment, I wanted to keep my thoughts and feelings to myself. They weren't for sale, not even for a penny. They weren't for sale for any price. I knew, however, that if we were to remain close friends I would have to eventually share my thoughts, my feelings and my longings with her. I enjoy friends like that, Lord. I love the closeness that sharing can bring. But sometimes interpersonal intimacy can be an unwelcome burden, dear God. The very thought of having to carry someone else's thoughts and feelings in addition to our own can sometimes be more than we can bear. And, knowing that others are having to carry my thoughts and feelings can be an additional burden as well. So, help me dear Lord, to cherish those moments when I can be lost in my own private reverie. But keep me from liking these private moments too much. I don't want to end up refusing pennies that could enrich my life by enjoying the feeling of closeness with others. I don't want to wake up some morning with my mind wonderfully brimming with private thoughts and having no one intimate enough in my life with whom these thoughts and feelings could and should be shared.

Finding Contentment

Dear God, one of the most disturbing four-letter words I know is the word 'more.' It seems that no matter how much of anything I possess I seem to want more of it. Whether it is money or food or a new pair of shoes. Having more of everything seems so very important to me these days. When I was younger I managed to get by with so much less than I now have but as I have grown older I find myself less and less content with less and more and more desirous of more. Where will all of this excessive desire lead me, O God? How much do I really need of all of these additional things? My appetite for more seems out of control. Everything I acquire becomes the minimum level for what I want next. I find myself moving from one fulfilled desire to the next unfulfilled one. Please curb my excessive appetite so I can find that sweet contentment I have somehow lost along the way. Help me to understand how less can really be more. Fill me with your divine presence so I won't be so tempted to fill myself with things that aren't very fulfilling. Help me to be content with less so I won't have to be so discontented with more.

Being Glad To Be Alive

I am so glad to be alive today Lord! I know this world is not perfect. People can sometimes be unbelievably cruel and life can sometimes be terribly harsh. However, when I think more seriously about it I am convinced that we live in a wonderful world, Lord. The rain comes and the unclean air is washed away. The sun sets each evening and we hear the same cricket-sounds that faith-filled people heard three thousand years ago when they sat by the evening's fires contemplating the mystery of God's wonderful presence in their lives. Miracles come and go like falling stars across the sky on a warm summer's night. Many of them go unrecognized but the ones we do see and witness renew our sense of your continued presence and caring. What a joy it is to see and witness these unexpected wonders. I am very glad I am alive today. It is a wonderful and fascinating world you have created for us. Thank you for the falling stars. I know as you catch them you will catch me too when I fall . . . even on a warm summer's night.

Our Wonderful World

Lord, this is a wonderful world you have made. I know there are all sorts of people who can temporarily make me think that this isn't so. But it is so. This is a wonderful world and scoundrels and hurtful people simply cannot change that fact. When you finished your creative work in the very beginning of time you said "It is good." You were overly modest I think. You should have said, "It is great!" Because that is what it is. It is great! I know that misery or misfortune sometimes distorts our perceptions. I know there are moments when my own frightening circumstances keep me from seeing clearly the beautiful world that is here for me. Help me to be more patient with my circumstances. Help me to trust and know that terrible moments have a way of changing and that perceptions also have a way of changing along with them. When those difficult moments come to me in my life, fortify my patience to do its magical work of bringing your wonderful world back into its beautiful focus again. I am convinced that a world like that is not justgood, dear God. It's great!

Vacation Time

"Sleep that knits back the raveled sleeve of care." Those were Shakespeare's words, dear Lord. But sometimes sleep is not enough. Sometimes we need more than sleep. A change of location. A change of schedule. A change of places and faces. A vacation. That wonderful time of year where ringing telephones disappear and we feel we are not needed by anyone at all in the entire world. A wonderful, carefree, low-blood-pressure time of life. Dear God, I pray that more of your children will have some of these carefree moments for their own sleeve repair. I have discovered that many important things in our lives can come unraveled in a very short time. There are not many moments in most of our days where we can completely avoid the demands and cries of needful people. Some of your children need a break before they break, O God. Please be with us during these moments of glorious rest as you have also been with us in our months of diligent labor. We know that most of us are not as eloquent as Shakespeare, but we certainly are as needy.

Being Carefree

I remember playing hooky from school when I was a young boy, Lord. It wasn't altogether what I thought it would be. I kept expecting the truant officer to grab me at any moment and drag me back to school where I would have to face the music and my transgression. I spent the entire day looking over my shoulder in fear. But the one good thing about that experience was having the entire day off. A day when I didn't have to be accounted for. A day when I didn't have to act responsibly. One day in my young life when I didn't have to try so hard to act mature and grown up. I still think about that day and I still remember those wonderful feelings I had of skipping school. I understand much better now the need in all of us to preserve that care-free spirit in us which can so easily be extinguished by living in such a care-full world. Dear Lord, it is not that I want to permanently play hooky from my responsibilities nor do I want to run away from being an adult. It is just that I don't want that carefree child in me to be completely neglected or abandoned either. Help me to not only smell the flowers as I go along in my life but help me to reach out and pick a few too, just like a young child would do. Maybe I won't have to face the music after all. Maybe I'll actually be able to hear some of it more clearly.

A Successful Person

I met a very successful person the other day, Lord. She was not a college-educated lady. She didn't own her own business nor was her name one that many people would readily recognize. She lived in a very small, rented apartment and her speech revealed her lack of formal education. She was not clever, ambitious, or very impressed with herself. In fact, it was the very absence of these qualities that made her so appealing to me. What she possessed, that drew people to her like a magnet, was her interest and total absorption in the lives of the people she encountered each day and the attitude she expressed to everyone she met was that she had all the time in the world for each of them. The truth is I am sure she did not have any more free time than the rest of us but she gave others the impression she did. I suppose the world, in general, would not define this woman as being a very successful person. But I see her that way, O Lord. She succeeded as a person. She succeeded as a human being. The more she thought about me the less I could resist thinking about her. There aren't very many people like this woman who are successful in this way anymore. She succeeded in getting my attention and if some people dare think of her as a failure, Lord, please help me to learn how to fail like her.

Happiness That Fits

Dear Lord, years ago when I earned only $10,000 a year I remember hoping and wishing that I might someday earn $20,000 a year. I recall feeling that life surely would be so much better for me and for my family if I could only earn $20,000 a year. I also remember, that when I finally did earn $20,000 a year, my life wasn't really that much better at all for me or my family. In fact, we spent everything we made and still found ourselves wanting more. The amount of my income kept increasing year after year. We spent everything we made and our life together as a family remained pretty much the same as it always had been. We were still living as if much of our happiness was somehow dependent on our income. It has taken me a number of years to learn, dear God, that I probably will never earn what I think is enough money. I will probably always want a little more. What a terrible trap to fall into, dear Lord. How much money is really enough? How much is too much? How much have I lost in life getting what I have gotten? Isn't it true that all of us have come into this world wrapped in a small basket and that we will all have to leave here some day in just a slightly bigger one? Dear God, keep us from working so hard in our trying to accumulate what will never quite fit in any basket we may select no matter what its size may be.

God's Day Off

This is the day after my day off from work, Lord. What a wonderful feeling it was, dear God, to have a day free from the cares and demands of life. A day of rest. A day of release from life's responsibilities. A day where I didn't have to answer to anyone else. But as our Creator and Protector, O God, you never have had that kind of day off have you? What a terrible world it would be, indeed, if you were to take a day off from us. All of our prayers would go unanswered. The House of Representatives and the Senate would have to rule without your presence being invoked in their assemblies. Divine miracles would end for the day. The universe would lose its supporting foundation for twenty-four hours. I cannot begin to imagine the misery we would all have to experience if you took time off from your job of supporting us. I am so glad you are always there when I need you. I am so relieved to know that when I slumber and sleep, you don't. I know it's been a long time since you have rested, Lord. The tranquility of our hearts are the ever-present

evidence of how well you are doing your job
. . . every day.

How A Good Memory Helps A Worrisome Heart

O God, what a terrible weight a person's worries can be. There aren't many things in life that weigh me down as much as do the things I worry about. My greatest problem, dear Lord, is not that I lack faith. I have plenty of faith and believe that faith can move mountains. I have seen that happen. My problem is not with my faith. My problem is with my memory. I keep forgetting how many mountains faith has moved and removed in my life. If I could remember more accurately I am certain I would worry less frequently. So, dear Lord, restore my memory. Bring to my mind the memories of those times when my faith in you replaced my tears in the middle of a dark night with the gladness of a sun-lit morning. Help me to recall the countless ways your presence has been felt in my life in both the good times and in the worrisome ones as well. Lord, I don't think I need a stronger faith. I just need a better memory.

Making Things Perfectly Clear

"It is as clear as black and white!" That's what she said to me, O God. But it didn't seem that clear to me at all. In fact, many things in life don't seem as clear and simple to me as they once were. The exceptions to the rules and the ambiguities of life seem to confront me on all sides more often than I can successfully sort them all out. I am amazed at how simple and straightforward things appear to some people and how complex and complicated they often appear to me. I am sometimes unsure whether I know and understand too much about life or whether I simply don't know and understand enough. Many people are so filled with intellectual arrogance that it feels to me as if they are playing a game of smoke and mirrors with the truth. Be patient with me, O God, while I try to sort out the many important issues of life that confuse and sometimes befuddle my thinking. Help me especially with those perplexing gray areas in my life, O Lord. I sincerely would like for more things to be simply black or white for me. I long for a greater certainty about many things but until I am able to obtain that certainty, please give me a generous spirit of humility so I don't come off as a know-it-all before this longed-for clarity comes to me.

When I Don't Know How To Pray

It is one of those moments, Lord, when I really feel tongue-tied. I greatly need and want to talk to you but I don't seem to have the right words with which to do it. In fact, I don't seem to have any words at all. I feel like a little child with a bad case of stage fright. I am full of things that need to be spoken: glorious things, happy things, and some things that are frightening and serious. Maybe I'm afraid that my lack of words would make me choose words that would sound trite or shallow. I am sure of one thing, O Lord. My silence right now is not a sign of my emptiness. I've got a whole lot more to say to you than I have the ability with which to say them. So, please be patient with me. Accept this quietness on my part as my attempt to put into words what you have already put into my heart.

When I Don't Know What To Ask For

    I don't want to be selfish when I pray to you, dear God. It seems that when I talk to others I think of those things I personally want or think I desperately need. But when I talk to you I really don't want you to do for me what I can easily do for myself. In my conversations with you, O Lord, I admit it has often been so much easier for me to pray for a miracle than to pray that I try harder to be or become a miracle for someone else. So, please forgive me when my prayers are not as neatly sorted out as they ought to be. It is very reassuring to me to know that good answers on your part do not require perfectly clear and articulate questions on mine.

When I Am In A Hurry

God, I don't know what to say to you right now. It's not that I don't have anything to say it's just that I don't have a whole lot of time in which to say it. I am in a terrible hurry today. I wish there was a kind of abbreviated prayer that would work in moments like these. Some short-hand prayer that would work for me and please you at the same time. I know you don't like to hear me talk this way. I know you much prefer those times when I speak to you without my eyes on the clock. I prefer those times too, O Lord. But this is just one of those days. I'm in such a hurry. Please hurry along with me.

Molehills And Mountains

Lord, I have never fully understood when little or relatively unimportant things should be expanded upon and when they shouldn't be. Sometimes I have been guilty of making mountains out of molehills when I shouldn't have. I have also missed other opportunities to expand on the good and important things that were quietly done in a corner which hadn't received any fanfare or attention at all. I want to get better at seeing these little things all around me which I can enlarge upon and learn to dismiss the other things that I should not make any larger than they already are. Help me to recognize the things that are a big deal in life and the other things that are not. I know that some of the things I enlarge upon wear me out with my worrying over them. I also know that the other things I have enlarged and expanded upon have refreshed and invigorated me. I think of a hand-written note of gratitude written to someone at a critical moment in their life. I think of a timely word of encouragement to a discouraged friend, or a gift of money given to tide someone over until their next check comes to them. All of these situations seem like such small things to some people, dear God, but they really seem like a big deal to me. They seem like mole hills that need to be recognized as mountains.

Changing Times And Changing Perceptions

Dear Lord, the other day I said to a young person: "I know how you feel. I was young once." What I said, O Lord, was the truth but it wasn't the entire truth. It is true that I was young once. But what was not true is the fact that I wasn't young now. I wasn't young today. I wasn't young in these trying times. Being young today isn't quite the same as being young when I was young. How could I fully have known how that young person felt today? When I was young, families still had their evening meals together and mothers worked only at home and they were able to talk with their children when they came home from school in the afternoon. When I was young, guns were something we went hunting with not something we used on one another. Sex was an experience we looked forward to after we were married not something we engaged in while we were getting ready for marriage. Dear God, I remember how it felt to be young once. I remember the world I was young in. But both my youth and that world are gone now. I am an older person in a world that has changed. I wish I could see the world today through more youthful eyes. I suppose I'll just have to trust the young to tell me how they feel about it. Perhaps someday when the young are my age they will say about me: "I know how he felt. I am old now too." And, of course, they will be both right and wrong.

There Ought To Be A Law

Dear Lord, she had been with the company longer than most of the people there. The promotion should have been hers. She had earned it. She was fully qualified for it but the promotion went to someone else. It went to a newcomer to the company. He had become a close friend with the boss. It was the old-boy network at work all over again. It was so unfair and cruel. O God, it seems to me there ought to be a law against such unjust and unkind behavior. But, maybe we can't write laws that require or guarantee moral behavior on our part. Maybe we can only write laws to prevent the expression of immoral behavior. I wish we could sometimes give goodness and morality a helping hand. There ought to be a law. Would decency look as good to us if it was legislated and forced by law? Maybe decency wouldn't appear so attractive to us if decency was the only choice a person could make in life. I know I would like it much better if people were nice to me because they wanted to be nice and not just because they were forced to be nice by a written law. I wish, somehow, that niceness and fairness were so commonplace among us that people would conclude that someone must have passed a law requiring such actions. However, I suppose if morality didn't come from our heart's deep desire, the law could never ever be able to put a pretty face on it.

Changing Along With Change

Dear Lord, I was thinking the other day of some things that no longer exist that used to be a part of my everyday life. Glass milk bottles were delivered to my front door. Two-by-four boards actually measured two inches by four inches. There were things I could buy for a penny. A movie ticket would allow me to sit through the movie for the second time on a Saturday afternoon. Typewriters. The list of course, could go on and on. These were the things that were around me when I was younger. They helped me to order and regulate my everyday life. But these things are gone now, O Lord. They have been replaced by other things that are said to be better, more reliable and efficient. More modern and up-to-date. Progress is certainly an unsettling experience, dear God. Progress is forcing me to find my milk in different places and to carry different amounts of money to pay for it when I finally find it. Please, O God, give me the patience to change graciously with all that is changing around me. Prevent me from boasting too much and too loudly about the things I cherished in my past. Keep me from making too many contemporary comparisons with the way things once were. Help me to understand that thinner boards can still a house make and that one viewing of a movie is probably just as good as seeing it twice, particularly if it is only half as good in the first place.

When I Am Envious

Dear God, I am aware of the fact that I am never envious of someone who makes less money than I do; has children who are less beautiful or talented than mine are; or who has a worse golf score than I have. My envy is most always directed toward someone who has something I want, but lack. It seems to me that my envy is really nothing more than covetousness. A form of greed. I want it all. I want what I already have and more. It isn't just that I lack something, it is that what I lack someone else already possesses and I want it. My envy is often just another form of theft. I am not sure I want it so that they will have less or whether I want it so I will have more. O Lord, my prayer to you is that you will restore in me a feeling of contentment. These envious feelings within me are robbing me of my contentment. Help me to rid myself of my desires for what others have so I can more fully enjoy the abundance of what I already have. I know for certain the price I am paying for wanting more is not worth the pain I am feeling for wishing for it. Lead me to that feeling of satisfaction that will keep me from wishing for someone else to possess less just so I could possess a little more.

Good Taste

I couldn't believe this young person I love so much actually chose to wear the clothes he was wearing. Baggy pants, a haircut that looked like the barber changed his mind halfway through the job of cutting it, and an earring that hung two inches below his earlobe. "This is a cool outfit," he said to me. Cool was not the word I would have chosen to describe it. His dog still loved him just as much as always and so did I, but it was clear to me that personal tastes in clothing and other things can differ greatly among people who deeply love one another. Help me to keep that point clearly understood in my mind, dear God. Help me to remember that it is our love for one another that binds us together not our similar tastes in music, food, clothing, or even those friends we choose to feel close to. Keep me from eroding other people's love for me by my insistence on their conforming to my taste in so many things. Help me to trust more fully that it is our love and positive regard for one another that should be relished and cherished not our fickle preferences for fashion. Help me to be more like that faithful old dog who never looks at a person's haircut at all but only sees the person who's wearing it.

Sincerely Wrong

No one could have faulted his sincerity, dear God. He wanted his children to be good children so he punished them severely every time they did something wrong. With every wrong step on their part his punishment grew more extreme. More harsh. The motivation for his cruelty was sincere enough. He simply wanted his children, above all else, to be good children even if he had to beat them into submissive goodness. But, dear Lord, are the motives that guide our actions in life the only basis for the judgment we should receive for what we do in life? Are good motives an adequate justification for bad conduct? Can any person ever be excused for doing something for someone's supposed good when that something ends up injuring or even destroying the other person in the process? I know you honor a sincere heart, O God, but isn't it possible to be sincerely wrong when we bring the entire sky down around a person's ankles with our so-called sincere intentions? Help me to be more sincere, dear God, but keep my sincere intentions from bringing unjustified pain to the people around me. Help me to not cripple my little children or others around me through my sincere but misguided efforts in guiding them to walk a good path in life. Prevent me from becoming a good parent in the worst sense of the term.

Forgetting Yourself

I forgot something the other day, dear God, that left me feeling very good. I forgot myself. For a few moments I was totally preoccupied with thinking about someone else and my own self was forgotten. Abandoned. Lost. Out of sight. Out of mind. I have to tell you, Lord, it was quite a wonderful experience indeed. I have heard of out-of-body experiences but this was an out-of-self experience. There was no thought of self-esteem, self-expression, or self-realization. There was no thought for the self-centered concerns that usually grip my every day. They were held at bay for a few moments and I discovered how wonderful it was to not have to carry the ponderous baggage of my over-inflated ego for awhile. I actually felt lighter. I felt as if I could carry another person's burdens so much easier when I wasn't so weighed down with my own load of self. I felt as if I could carry twice as much with half the effort. Wouldn't it be wonderful, dear God, if all of us could learn to do this better? Think of the kind of world we would be able to create and help carry if we could learn this valuable lesson. In this new kind of world the very moment when I would be reaching out to lift someone else's burden some other selfless self would be reaching out to carry mine. What a wonderful world that would surely become. Everyone forgetting themselves only to be remembered by someone else in turn.

What A Saint

It seems to me, dear God, that to not strike someone back when we have been wounded unjustly by that other person takes considerable restraint. To not even speak of that injustice to another is also truly a sign of unusual grace. To not even think at a later time of that wound so unfairly inflicted, I believe is the mark of a true saint. Maybe that's why there are so few saints in circulation these days. It is my thoughts dear Lord, not just my deeds, that rob me of sainthood. How often I diminish myself by diminishing others in my private thoughts of them. I reduce my own spiritual stature, inch by inch, by reducing others in my mind. As others become smaller and smaller in my own thoughts of them I seem to stand less tall myself. It seems the more I look down on others the easier I make it for them to look down on me. It is not at all surprising to me that no one has ever accused me of being a saint.

Angry Words

I wish I could have recalled those words I spoke in anger, Lord. They slipped out of my mouth before I could stop them. Even as I heard them fall from my lips I knew they were the wrong words. They were the worst words I could have spoken. I saw her face. She looked as though I had slapped her. I had. I had slapped her with my words. Thoughtless, venom-filled words. I could see that the sting of them went to the very marrow of her soul. I knew I had done more than surface damage. Those careless remarks were the wounding instruments of pain that I knew would linger long after the actual words were forgotten. Help me, O God, to build a conscious barrier around my hurtful speech so that when I feel angry these awful words will not easily leap over the fence of good reason and sensitive kindness. Help me to remember that, like an arrow shot into the air, an unkind word that is spoken can never be taken back. Help me when I am upset with someone else to not just stop counting to ten before I speak. Supply me with as many larger numbers as it takes to enable me to speak words that will bless rather than wound or burden someone else's life for years to come.

Savers And Non-Savers

Dear God, I have noticed that some people are savers and others like to throw things away. It seems almost impossible to change the one kind of person into the other. But, dear Lord, it also seems that what we choose to save or throw away defines the kind of person we are. The person, for instance, who saves old string and rubber bands is a very different kind of person than the parent who saves every work of art their children created and proudly gave to them in their childhood. A person who throws away last month's magazine subscription is a very different kind of person than the one who discards old friends as if they weren't important anymore. O God, I wonder what kind of things I have been keeping and what kind of things I have been throwing away all these years. I wonder if I have discarded what I should have held on to. I cannot help but ask myself, dear God, whether the clutter of the so-called important things I have saved in my life has actually kept me from seeing more clearly the things I should have discarded from my life. I miss some of those valuable things like honor, self-respect, and personal integrity that I have sometimes carelessly thrown away in the past. I am also bothered by other things like ambition, pride, and my own selfish agenda that I have kept and saved all rolled up with a big red ribbon around them. Treasured objects thought to be worth keeping. O God, keep my life from being cluttered with the things that are not important. Keep me from discarding those things that are. Give me the wisdom to clearly know the difference between the two.

Letting Go

Lord, I simply cannot go to sleep. It is midnight and my mind is still racing like a runaway locomotive. I am reworking the events of today and have already begun worrying about the ones tomorrow. I want to let go and give them over to you to carry for awhile but I simply cannot resist worrying over them a little longer. I'm having a difficult time letting go and trusting you more these days. I know you never slumber or sleep so why am I so intent on staying awake? I have read stories of saints being able to fall asleep in the midst of violent storms. I want that kind of peaceful sleep, Lord. It's raining pretty hard down here right now. It is not good sleeping weather. I feel like I should worry a little bit longer, but frankly, I don't have much strength left for doing it. The wonderful thing about weariness O Lord, is that it makes trusting you so much easier to do. I wish I had become more weary more quickly.

The Bond Of Love

They were so different from each other, Lord, and yet they had been married to one another for over 50 years. She liked to stay up late. He went to bed early. They voted for different political candidates. They liked different food. However, there was one thing they both agreed on: they loved each other! It was their love for each other that bound them together not their agreement on dozens of issues one might expect would divide them. I wish we all could understand that, O God. Those of us who claim to be a part of your family are so divided and separated from each other on so many issues. We even wear distinctive names to identify ourselves so people will not be confused and think that somehow we are really connected to each other. We write and say ugly things about one another. We leave the impression that we are enemies not spiritual brothers and sisters. We are so devoted to our beliefs that we have no affection or devotion left over to give to one another. I think we could survive our differences if our love for one another was strong enough. Wouldn't it be wonderful if we could love one another enough to close the gaps our intellectual beliefs have created? What a marriage that would be. One worth celebrating indeed.

Cleanse Me

Dear God, it seems to me that living the religious life is very much like washing the back of one's neck. The back of our neck is almost impossible for us to see. It is invisible to us. Being able to wash what we cannot see is very much like trying to cope with life itself. We can neither see or understand much of it very clearly either. I am so glad you can see the back of my neck, O God. The very part of me which I cannot see very well. Please cleanse all of me, dear Lord, even those places within me that I do not see or understand very clearly. I don't want to be only clean in those places where everyone can easily see. I want to be clean all over so I won't have to be surprised or embarrassed when you check my neck . . . and my heart.

A True Friend

There are few things in life, O God, as wonderful and treasured as a true friend. A true friend is like a comfortable pair of old shoes. A friend just simply fits well. No matter how bent out of shape we can sometimes get, a friend will always find a way to fit into our changing moods and temperament. A friend will see the best in us even when we don't see it ourselves. A friend will tell us the truth about ourselves in a way that doesn't injure or scar or discourage. A friend is a person we would let pack our parachute and a friend is a person we would literally go through all kinds of living hell with. Falling in love, O Lord, is sometimes described as an instantaneous experience. But true friendship seems to not be the result of a fall at all. Instead, I think two people have to travel a great distance with one another to create a friendship. Making a friend takes a lot of time and patience. Perhaps that is why true friendships are so rare and fit and feel so well once they are finally formed.

Grace Under Fire

Lord, I truly love it when I see someone handle a person's bad attitude with grace. I think the worst thing in all the world is to see someone who is ill-tempered run into another person who is similarly afflicted. It is like two freight trains on a collision course. But when I see someone skillfully deflect another person's hurtful accusations or cutting remarks with the gentleness of a surgeon removing a thorn from a throbbing finger, it is like witnessing one of life's holy and sublime moments. It seems to me that to resist the temptation to get even in nastiness toward another is one of the great signs of character. Please help me, O God, to try harder to get even with others for goodness sake. Turn me into a surgeon of good-will that removes pain wherever and whenever I find it and prevents me from becoming a runaway train that continually creates collisions in the world around me.

Becoming Sensitive To A Grieving World

O God, why do such terrible tragedies have to occur before we are willing to come together as a family of concerned people? Why do people have to die in some awful way before the rest of us are compelled to give and to live the right way? Why does so much pain have to be felt before our generous healing efforts are felt and expressed to others? Some of us do not give very generously of ourselves until there is some dramatic or urgent request made for a compassionate response on our part. But what about the undramatic, every-day kind of need that is continuously in our midst, dear God, that occurs with regularity all around us which captures no one's special attention? It is so easy to become immune to tragedy when we routinely brush up against it every day of our life. There is such an ordinariness to much of the pain we see every day that make us blind to so much of it. We become so unresponsive to human hurting in general that it takes an unbelievably horrifying event to finally awaken us to do the good we should have been doing all along. God, please make me more sensitive to the daily painful grieving all around me so that I won't require something even more terrible to get my full attention.

Becoming Satisfied With Less

God, why is it that if we have two children and three oranges each child seems to want two of them? It doesn't seem to change very much with adults either except that the oranges turn into money and other expensive things and the little children turn into spoiled older children who often confuse what they want with what they think they really need. How much do we really need anyway, Lord? Could we be just as happy with less? Are my creature comforts turning me into a creature that keeps demanding more and more comforting? Am I so busy getting more than my fair share of oranges that I cannot even see those who have no oranges at all? God, the simple truth is it really hurts having so much extra when I see people who don't have much of anything at all. Do you suppose, dear Lord, if I could learn to become satisfied with less that my heart would be blessed with so much more?

Resting . . . One Day Of The Week

". . . and on the seventh day the Lord rested!" Were you tired, Lord, or did you just stop working for some other reason? The work you did on those six days was pretty wonderful but I think your effort on the seventh day was just as important as what you did all week long. I am glad you set that resting example for us. It is so much easier to stay busy and preoccupied with creating our own narrow worlds than it is to rest and reflect on the kind of world you would like us to create in the first place. Maybe that's our problem. Maybe the reason our world isn't working as well as it could for more of us is because too many of us have put the seventh day out to work for us. Perhaps things won't work so well for us in the first six days when there is no rest and reflection supporting them on the seventh. How can we expect to be meaningfully creative, O Creator, on less rest than you had? Lord, shut us down for at least one day a week so we can have the energy and the perspective to follow in your creative footsteps the other six work days you gave in labor before you finally rested from it yourself.

Shoes Tell The Story

Dear Lord, it's amazing how much you can tell about a person's life by looking at their shoes. When someone is in love their shoes are always clean and polished. However, when a person has been rejected or disappointed in love their shoes often become dirty and unpolished. There is a who-cares-how-they-look about those shoes. There are a lot of dirty shoes around these days, O Lord. A lot of dusty shoes and lonely and unloved faces which seem to go together. It breaks my heart, O God to think that there isn't enough love to go around for everyone. Is someone hoarding love and taking it to some far off place? Has some of the extra love and affection been devilishly diverted to some private cul-de-sac for someone's selfish enjoyment? The picture of so many unpolished shoes is a very discouraging thing to behold. Please help me to be more generous in my loving of others so I can brighten some people's faces and perhaps their shoes as well.

Money Talks Eloquently

Dear God, a group of children had a bake sale the other day to help pay their way to winter camp. I put a $20-dollar bill in their cash box and took a donut to eat. I thought to myself: "I wonder where this $20-dollar bill has been during its lifetime and I wonder what it had purchased on its journey?" I couldn't help but think that it might have bought a drink at a bar or have been a part of a payment for an illegal drug purchase. Maybe it had traveled to a gambling casino and had been won and lost several times in some game of chance before it made its way to my pocket. I wondered to myself whether it had ever served some noble purpose in its life's journey from one hand to another. I couldn't help but wonder whether it had been handed to a homeless person or perhaps put into some offering plate in a religious service somewhere. I thought to myself that if this $20-dollar bill could talk, what stories would it tell? Then it dawned on me. Money does talk. It talks very loudly. Those children are going to come back from winter camp thrilled, inspired, and full of wonderful conversations about the noble things they had learned and experienced. It is true. Money does talk, dear God. I understand that. I am beginning to see that it depends on each one of us to make sure that our money always says the right thing whether it is put in a youth-camp box or in some other special place we choose to put it.

Creatures Of Habit

Dear God, I have discovered that one of the most difficult things in life to accomplish is to do something, anything at all, for the very first time. Yes, doing anything for the first time is difficult but doing it for the second time is a little easier. Doing it for the third time is a piece of cake. And, doing it for the fourth time is a walk in the park. How quickly we become creatures of habit, dear Lord. Both good ones and bad ones. I suppose, then, the place where we have to be so very careful is at the beginning. Please help me to start out right, Lord, in the things I choose to do in life. Get me off to a good start so I can end up with a good finish. If things are going to get easier and easier for me as I continue doing them then I want to get better at doing the right things in the first place. I certainly do not want to become more and more efficient at doing the wrong things in life. Please, dear God, help me to do the very best things in life the very first time I set out to do them and then continue to walk with me in the park.

Older People

Dear God, I would like to talk to you about elderly people. We sometimes refer to elderly people as senior citizens because we don't want to sound offensive in the language we use to talk about them. We don't want to sound as if we are being critical or negative when we speak of them. But some people really are old, dear God. That is what they are. They are old. They are elderly. They are advanced in years. It seems to me that when we use language that disguises what people actually are that we are treating them as if they don't actually exist or that the form of their existence is repugnant in some awful way. We sometimes act as if 'old' is a four-letter word instead of a three-letter one. Help us to remember, dear God, that your name is a three-letter word too. I know that being older has its special problems but so does being younger. Being older has some advantages as well. Those frustrating battles with youthful passions and ambitious struggles for personal success have usually been tempered over time leaving the older ones among us with a sense of quiet contentment or at least a sense of negotiated resignation with their lot in life. I wish, dear God, that more of us would make this kind of peace with our lives earlier than we do. I really do love older people, O Lord. I hope I live long enough to become one.

Time On My Hands

I didn't think about it very much when I was young, O Lord. It was a non-issue with me then. It was something I had plenty of. There was a whole lot more of it ahead of me than there was behind me. We tend not to spend much time thinking about our surpluses in life. It is what we lack in life that seems to fill more of our thoughts than what we have plenty of. It is when the container is almost empty that we begin thinking of its dwindling contents not when it is completely full. I am thinking a whole lot more about time lately, dear God. I am thinking more and more about the amount of time I have left to live. There is a certain sadness about our mortality. The older we get the more it seems that a new kind of greed slips into our thinking; the greed of wanting a little more time for me and for the people I love. More time for personal growth and understanding. More time to appreciate time itself as a declining commodity in my life. Our time here is far too short, O God. There is so much more time behind me now than there is ahead of me. It is certainly more of an issue with me these days than it once was. But Lord, keep me from being so concerned about the little time I have left that I forget to remember and cherish the wonderful time I have already had and am still trying hard to have and enjoy to the fullest!

We Are All Unfinished Symphonies

I love the fact, Lord, that we are all unfinished symphonies. There is so much potential in each of us but so much of that potential is seldom fully realized. I know that I am unfinished, Lord. It is clear that your work in me is not completed yet. I suppose that this fact should encourage me to be more patient with others. I need to remember that others are symphonies too and that they are unfinished ones just like me. Please help me to remember this the next time I am tempted to be critical or unforgiving. Help me to remember how patient you have been with me when my life has been full of discordant sounds. Keep working on me Lord to find that beautiful lost chord that still may allude me or not be fully developed within my soul. Restore that chord's harmony in me. Complete in me the symphony you want written with my life. The world has lost much of its good music, today God. Help me to be one of those who can help find some of it once again. Help us all to become fully finished symphonies. I like the sound of that. I cannot help but think that this thought must be sweet music to your ears as well, O God.

Being A Father

Father's Day is only a couple of days away, O God. I'm spending a lot of time thinking about my father who helped shape my understanding of the important things in my life and also about my sons who are fathers as well and how they have shaped my understanding of me. My father wasn't a very emotional person, Lord, except when he was upset with us children. I think I have done a little better with my children by sharing with them my personal feelings, even when I am not being upset with them. I love watching my sons being fathers to their children. I see their unabashed affection toward their children. How unrestrained they are with their concern for their needs. How empathetic they are with their understanding of where their children are coming from in those troubled times they sometimes have. How unconditional in the expressions of their love. Good children have a marvelous way of often making us fathers look so much better than we sometimes deserve to look. It has been a privilege for me to teach my children about the good life and, in turn, to learn from them too when they teach their children about the good life for them as well. When I stop and mull that thought over for a moment I think that is about the very best Father's Day gift any dad could ever ask for.

Running Out Of Time

Dear God, I used to think when I was a young man that tomorrow would never come. I never gave much thought to the fact that I would someday have thinning hair. I didn't think I would ever stand breathless at the top of a long flight of stairs or that I would have more stored-up memories behind me than unfulfilled dreams and ventures ahead of me. Well, here I am Lord, standing firmly planted in middle age with a whole lot less hair and a lot more memories than I would really like to admit having. Where has all the time gone? Who crept in while I was napping and painted a wintry scene on my head? I don't mind so much the idea of growing older but what I really do not like so well is the idea of being old. I don't want to be one of those old-timers who are guilty of warming up old thoughts and ideas like last night's leftovers. Deliver me, Lord, from the awful temptation of liking the sound of my voice too dearly and from broadcasting tiresome stories of the past to ears that are too polite to not listen one more time. I really don't want friends and family who are trying to run away from me with their eyes. Keep me young at heart and young in my mind. Tomorrow has finally come for me, dear God, but please disguise it as today. That young man whom I remember so well is now disguised as someone else. It amazes me how quickly we run out of our tomorrows and run out of our young men as well.

Feeling Young Again

I saw two young newlyweds the other day, dear God. They were so filled with love for each other. The energy they felt for one another was tremendous. One couldn't help but feel a huge part of what they were feeling. It was captivating and wonderful. It made all of us who were with them feel young and alive again. I couldn't help but wonder whether this was the way it once was for the rest of us. How easy it is to allow the passing of time to dull our passions. How easy it is to slip into the comfort of a routinized, passionless, existence in which form sometimes replaces content. I know what I felt when I saw that young couple. I want that glow back in my life again and the youthful vigor for life that goes along with it.

Twenty Four Hours To Live

Lord, someone said to me the other day: "What would you do if you were suddenly to learn that you only had one day left to live?" I think, dear God, there are some things I definitely would not do. I would not purchase anything on the installment plan. I wouldn't join a Book of the Month Club. I wouldn't purchase a bunch of green bananas. I wouldn't register in a program to improve my vocabulary or communication skills. When time is scarce we dismiss many of the luxuries we can enjoy when it isn't. When time is short we are abruptly thrust into thinking of disappearing minutes, not declining years. I think, dear Lord, I wouldn't waste a single minute speaking mean or hurtful words. Rationed time is so valuable. I think my speech would begin to sound like holy benedictions. I think my words would turn to healing, to comforting, and to honoring. Family and friends would be feverishly caressed with expressions of grateful appreciation for the countless joy-filled moments that seldom get acknowledged when we live with the sense of an unlimited future. My shyness at revealing my heart's truest feelings toward others would surrender to a candor born of shrinking opportunities to leave a part of my heart behind. I think, dear God, that in those last 24 hours I would discover, afresh, what my most valued life's treasures were. I would live in a hurry; the way I should have lived all along.

The Theft Of Childhood

I spoke to some girls in a juvenile detention facility the other day, Lord. One teenage girl had already murdered three people in her young life. Another had given birth to a child with another one soon to arrive. She had no husband. These girls were worldly-wise and hardened beyond what you would expect from children so young. How sad I felt for them. Our society is creating urban guerrillas out of people who should be children. They should be children with a sense of innocence and a feeling of softness in their hearts. They should be children who should know far less than they already know about the awful side of life. What a terrible theft has taken place. These children have been robbed of their most precious moments of life, their childhood. The early choices they have made have deprived them of the care-free experiences that help people feel good about themselves and about the world around them. My heart aches, dear God, for those calloused hearts in children's bodies. Please soften my heart towards them so I can help soften theirs.

The Divine Operator

O God, how often I have prayed for you to open some door for me or to make an important event happen or to not happen in my life. I have treated you like a heavenly telephone operator expecting you to provide for me some critical information I could have actually found for myself. I have expected you to take responsibility for my life when I should have taken responsibility for it myself. O Lord, it is so easy to just dial for help and assistance from you instead of taking productive or helpful action on my own. I know that taking action means risking taking the blame too if things don't work out so well. Perhaps that is what frightens me. It means going out on a limb in the face of frightening circumstances. It means inching away from the safety of the trunk of a tree, as it were. I know in my heart, however, that going out on the limb is where all the best fruit is. I know that the greatest blessings in life are located out and away from the safety of dependent living. I suppose there is no way I can have it both ways: a no-risk guarantee in life and the bountiful blessings of a fulfilled and fruitful life experience that comes from taking chances. Taking risks. So, the next time you get a panic call for help from me, please don't answer on the first ring. Give me what I really need most, more experience with picking fruit in scary places. I know that if I am in desperate trouble and really in need of help in a hurry that I can always call you collect.

Having An Easy Conversation

It is a wonderful experience, dear God, to get a phone call from someone who makes communicating an easy and pleasurable experience. It is so wonderful to talk to someone who carefully listens and understands what is not always spoken in words and who has the ability to complete my spoken sentence before it is put it into actual clearly understood language. I am never disappointed when I talk to you, O God. Bottling my feelings up deep inside me became the way I once chose to deal with those kind of painful, lonely experiences in my life. I was always the person with the big winsome smile on his face so no one ever suspected that the 'outside Larry' was any different from the 'inside Larry.' But it was, indeed, very much different on my inside and I knew it. No one ever chose to ask me whether there was any difference between these two Larry's so I never volunteered any further information to them. That practice sometimes continues for me even to this present moment. I have found that it is easier for me to just make accommodations to life's painful circumstances by just smiling at the world around me and moving on through them. I have often come to you with gladsome words and sometimes with painful ones. Sometimes I have come to you with mutterings that cannot even be converted into real or sensible language. I am always so grateful for the way in which you listen and complete my sentences which haven't always been very clearly spoken. I am glad for the mercy and grace that you give me in those moments when it has been difficult for me to be merciful toward myself. I am glad when you have continued to love me even when I haven't loved myself very much. I am grateful for your willingness to keep on listening to the same appeals that have fallen on your ears from my lips over and over again. So, for all of us who stammer with urgent and inarticulate words that desperately need to be spoken and for those of us who need to talk and need to know that someone is listening, thank you for hearing what we have said and for what we tried to say but didn't quite know how to say it.

Heaven, The Answer For An Unfair World

Life is so often unfair, dear Lord. I look around and see good and decent people suffering grave injustices and heartaches while those who are self-serving and ruthless get ahead and prosper. It doesn't make sense to me. There ought to be some cosmic law against this, God. One would think that life would provide rewards more commensurate with deeds. A system of equivalent retribution where the rain of tragedy and suffering would only fall on the unjust not on the just as well. But, alas, the righteous are sometimes more unjustly rained upon than are the unrighteous. This is so disheartening. So discouraging. Perhaps all the unfairness we experience in this life is a good argument for the existence of an afterlife in some far off heaven. This thought helps to restore a small sense of fair-play in a world that isn't very fair at all. I think one of the nicest thoughts about having the notion of a heaven, dear God, is that it can be a place where the good, the righteous, and the just will never have to worry again about the rain. Until all of that is revealed more fully to me in some far off moment in my life, I will just be content with carrying an umbrella!

God Is A Good Habit

I noticed the other day, O Lord, that I always put my right shoe on first when I dress in the morning. Never my left shoe. Always my right one. I don't even think much about it anymore. Habit simply has taken over and before I know it I am fully dressed, shoes and all. It makes me stop and think of how many other unthinking, habitual things I do each day. I brush my teeth in the same way. I take my vitamins and medications in ritual order. I drive to work on the same streets and dodge the same pot-holes each day without a single thought of the familiar scenery I pass along the way. Habit, the art of reducing the once-important things in life to the level of ritualized routine. Have I done that to you too, Lord? Have I reduced you to an obligatory, perfunctory sign-on and sign-off acquaintanceship? I don't want to lose the freshness and excitement we have had together through the years. I don't want to get from here to there each day without being fully aware of your meaningful presence along the way. I don't want to dodge the pitfalls and pot-holes of life without realizing that it is your constant encouragement that guides me around those potentially hurtful dangers. I don't suppose I'll ever put my shoes on again in the morning without smiling when I pick up my right shoe. Help me to smile, too, when I dodge a difficult situation in life because I have formed the good habit of having you close by my side every day, all the way, just as I have done over and over and over again.

I Believe In Miracles

Someone asked me the other day, Lord, whether I believe in miracles. I was a bit hesitant in knowing how to respond at first because this person is the kind of person who believes that getting the last good piece of chocolate pie in a restaurant falls clearly in the realm of the miraculous. I have always felt in my heart, O God, that miracles have to do with far more sublime issues of life than with matters of puddings and deserts. I have to admit, too, that I am not very convinced by the miraculous claims of perspiring, so-called healing preachers on television who shout "Heal! Heal!" just before they make their appeal for people to send in money to them. But, do I believe in miracles, God? Do I believe that your power still accomplishes what our own limited powers cannot? Do I believe that the word 'coincidence' is simply a word we give for unusual occurrences when we don't have the faith or the courage to admit that you are actually still at work in our lives? Yes! Yes! Yes! Yes to all of these questions! Believing in miracles is my way of saying: "I know you are still at work in this world and you and your spirit are still in charge of things down here." Believing in miracles is my way of keeping my arrogance and smugness in check. It is my way of acknowledging that you, who started the universe in the very beginning of time, can still get each one of us jump-started today in miraculous ways. I believe that you, who created life out of nothing, can still re-create new life today in those of us who feel like nobodies. I suppose, dear Lord, that once people start believing in miracles that they will probably begin seeing miracles in the strangest of places. Even, I'm sure, on chocolate pie racks in restaurants.

Seeing Miracles

Lord, did you really divide the scary waters so the children of Israel could pass through to the other side and escape from the Egyptians? I mean, did it really happen that way? Just between you and me, is that story for real? And all those other stories too: ax-heads which floated on the water; the sun standing still at noon; dead people rising and walking around town. Were they all for real? Did they all happen the way they were reported to have happened? I have to tell you, God, it is not easy to live in a world which says: "What you see is what you get." It is not easy to believe in things you cannot quite see or quite get. I'm having a hard time seeing many believable miracles around me these days. Maybe you are actually sending them and I'm just not getting them. I certainly hope you don't get tired of sending them before I can get better at seeing them.

Miracles

Dear God, thank you for the miracle you sent me the other day. It was completely unexpected. It was totally unexplainable. It was so very uplifting. I have to be honest with you, O Lord, I haven't always been so open to seeing miracles. I have always believed in ancient Bible miracles. I believe in the manna which fell from heaven to feed the Israelites in the desert. I believe in the walls which fell down when Joshua blew his trumpet near the city of Jericho. I have always believed in these historical biblical miracles but I have a much harder time believing in the everyday miracles people talk about today. Maybe I have seen too many people trivialize the miraculous. I have to admit, dear Lord, I was beginning to believe that there were no more honest-to-goodness miracles left for us today. I was beginning to believe that miracles were only historical facts not contemporary ones. So, thank you for the miracle you sent me the other day. I am also learning that when one sees one honest-to-goodness miracle that it helps us to see many others around us at the same time. I don't expect to see a miracle every day, Lord, but I'll tell you one thing for sure, the miracle I just witnessed this week has caused me to look for more to come and the next time I actually see one I won't be quite so surprised when one happens in my presence again.

Elevating The Obvious

Dear God, it is so easy to have great faith in the big events of life and to have such little faith in the small ones. I can easily see Moses dividing the Red Sea and Jesus bringing Lazarus back to life again. Big things. These kinds of wondrous happenings are easy for me to believe. But it is the small and simple things in life that make me wonder the most and which test my faith the greatest. Believing that a soft reply is better than a bombastic one. Believing that unselfishness is the ultimate road to happiness, not a me-first outlook on life. Believing that going the second mile gladly and willingly is what makes us feel good all over about going the first one in the first place. Believing that granting forgiveness to another is the best guarantee that it probably will be reciprocated to us by someone down the road in the future. Dear God, I wish it was as easy to believe in the obvious as it is to believe in the incredible. Help me to understand, dear Lord, that restoring the pieces of someone's broken heart is just as miraculous and wonderful as dividing the waters of a great sea. Help me to believe, O God, that every time I give a piece of my life to someone else I bring a little more of that other person's life back to him again as well. God, help me to make the obvious in life more incredible.

God, Our Security

Lord, in so many ways I liked it much better when my world consisted of simple truths such as: two plus two equals four and my dad is smarter and tougher than your dad. Things seemed so crystal-clear to me then. No ambiguities. No subtleties. No ifs, ands, and buts. No subtile nuances surrounding everything important that I am forced to think about in my day-to-day world. It was such a safe and secure world in those once-upon-a-time moments in my past. I think about those times often. If I was frightened or perplexed about anything at all my mother or father would sort things out and clarify them for me. Everything seemed to fit so nicely and comfortably in the childhood of my neat and orderly life. Most of my bumps and bruises were minor ones because of the carefully cushioned environment my parents provided me. But not anymore. Not many things seem as clear to me as they once were. There seems to be more than two sides to every question and issue that arise these days. Every truth statement has to be carefully qualified. More than ever before my life seems to be filled with ifs, ands, and buts. I used to have a security blanket. Now, I just have a blanket. Things no longer add up in the simple ways they once did. In times like these I feel as if I need a mother and father close by, dear God, but my parents are gone now. What I am trying to say, O Lord, is that I need someone I can count on to simplify and clarify my life. I need someone like you. I know you are smarter and tougher than anyone's dad. I have never quite gotten over the feeling that I need someone who is.

On My Knees

I was on my knees the other day, O Lord. On my knees in prayer. That's the way my mother taught me how to do it . . . on my knees. I have learned as I have grown older that when I cannot stand on my own two feet in life that it is much easier and more rewarding to face life on my knees. I have also learned that we are all pretty much the same height as one another when we are on our knees. I have learned that I can see life much more clearly from my knees and that I feel so much stronger when I am kneeling. God, help me to remember and to trust that in those times of my life when I feel that I cannot stand tall that I can kneel tall. That when I cannot rise to the occasion I can kneel to it. Help me to understand that wonderful things are accomplished in life not by people of great height but by people of great depth. I am glad that my mother understood that.

Angels On Earth

Lord, I heard some angels sing the other night! Yes I did. They were real angels. Of course I know they were really little children dressed up to look like angels for a Christmas program, but they were truly angels to me. They were so completely absorbed in the story they were telling that I found myself joyously believing all of it. I felt myself being lifted to a higher place. I found myself singing with them the words: "Glory to God in the highest." And I meant it. I meant every word of it. In that magical moment it had stopped being a children's play for me. It had become life. Real life. I guess that's what authentic angels do, isn't it Lord. They lift us above the ordinary. They bring a big dose of heaven right down to earth where we really need it. I want to be an angel to someone, Lord. I want to be a part of someone else's transformation. Whisper in my ear your celestial song so I can sing it to some person who really needs a lift, an experience with the transcendental.

I don't want to lose what I felt the other night. It was heavenly.

When To Look Up

I believe, dear God, in the truth once spoken by the Psalmist when he said: "He maketh me to lie down!" I believe that when we are made to lie down by life's sometimes crippling circumstances that there is no other direction for us to look in that moment but to look up. It is really a shame, dear Lord, that we have to be forced to lie down before we feel the need or the ability to look up. I can't help but feel you would like us to look up before we are forced to lie down. I am sure you would prefer that we look up to you because we wanted to not because we felt we needed to. Surely our heart-felt desire for you is infinitely more pleasing to you than is our desperate need for you in those calamitous moments that life delivers to us along our way. I am convinced that you will gladly respond to both our loving desire as well as to our desperate need for you when they occur to us but I can imagine how much more satisfying our burning heart of love must be to you than is our burning sense of urgency. God, help me to look to you while I am standing tall so I won't seem like such a stranger to you when I am lying down. Help me to be one of your best friends while I am on my feet so I won't have to be introduced to you, as if for the first time, when I am not.

Gaining My Senses

Dear Lord, the other day I met a woman who couldn't see. She had a close friend who couldn't hear. On the same day I visited a person who had no feelings in her body from her neck down because of a serious injury she had experienced years earlier in her life. Three people cut off from the world of sensations in very significant ways. And, yet, they didn't show or sense any overwhelming loss as they encountered the world they greatly enjoyed around them. They used the working parts of their bodies to fully absorb their surroundings. Physically, they possessed so much less than I did and yet they appeared to enjoy life so much more than I did on a daily basis. On the surface they seemed to be cut off from the world I could see and hear and touch, but in truth they were much more tuned in to it than I was. Dear God, I am not praying that I be given less in order that I might gain more. I am simply praying that you would help me to use my eyesight, my hearing, and my capacity to feel your wonderful world to its fullest. Help me to see with more than just my eyes. Help me to hear the words that are not even spoken. Help me to feel the things that no fingers can touch. I don't want my having more to leave me enjoying less. I simply want my more to leave me with enough. Enough for you. Enough for others. Enough even for me.

The Rat Race

Dear God, I was in a meeting the other day and someone said out loud: "How do we get out of this rat race in life?" Someone else in the room quickly responded by saying: "Stop being a rat!" There is so much truth in what that person said, dear God. We create so much of our own misery and weariness in life by being what we don't want to be and by doing what we really do not want to be doing. Help me, dear God, to stop blaming others for my own fatigue and tiredness. Help me to understand that so much of this weariness is of my own making. Help me to see more clearly what a heavy burden a bad attitude can create for us or how the compromising of our integrity can add weight to our beleaguered soul. Remind me again of how much easier it really is to carry twice the load with half the effort when our heart or spirit is right within us. I am not asking for a lighter load I am just asking for a better spirit with which to carry the one I already have. I know that at the end of a hard day that almost everyone will be tired. But, I also know that not everyone will be miserable. I know that tiredness is the burden the body bears but that it is misery that the heart carries. Lighten my heart, O God, so my body will not complain when it has done a hard day's work.

Hurrying To Nowhere

I heard the doctor say to her: "I'm sorry. The illness you have is terminal." Terminal illness. What an awful expression that is, dear God. The sound of it is so frightening. So devastating. So completely without any soft cushion to it at all. And when we stop to think about it for a moment it is so deceiving as well. Terminal illness never quite means that all illness is terminal at all, as if there was some point in time when illness itself will be over, finished, and gone. It means that the person is terminal not the illness. That the person will come to a point when their life will be over. That one's life will be finished and gone. However, dear Lord, I have seen some terminally ill people who did not think their life was finished or over at all. In fact, some of these remarkable people didn't begin to live until someone told them they were going to die. They discovered their greatest joy was not in striving or attaining some great place in life but, rather, in coming to appreciate the profound pleasures they had all around them but which they had not been seeing or recognizing for a very long time. Beautiful flowers. Abiding friendships. Soulful music. And those little children that had been coming in and out of their lives for years but had not really been seen or appreciated as they should have been all along. Those simple things in life. The truly important things that easily get sacrificed and reduced by all of those less important things. Dear God, help me to learn how to live before someone tells me I am going to die. If anything has to be terminal in my life let it be my overly ambitious striving for things that neither last nor deeply feed my soul. Keep me from being too much in a hurry to find what I could have found so much sooner if I had just learned to be more fully alive a little more quickly.

Teenagers

I read somewhere the other day, dear Lord, that the word 'teen' in 'teenager' means: troublesome, grief, vexation, and anger. That definition, O God, must have been written by a parent. By an older adult. What a grim view of such a delightful period in one's life. What a potentially wonderful period of time it can be between the 13th and 19th years of our life. It isn't just a time for acne and unbridled hormones. Teenage rebellion and disrespect for limits is not at all the only description of what can take place during these seven terrific years. It is a wonderful time of expanding independence and self-reliance. A time of discovering how unique we all are. So like and yet so unlike either of our parents. A time of testing what we have been told in the past to see if it truly fits with what we are actually experiencing in the world around us. A brief moment to explore and get acquainted with the feelings and emotions within us that will serve as a guide and counsel for us in those decision-making moments to come in our life. This time in our life passes so quickly for these young ones, dear God. The relative carefree moments of teenage life are gone for them almost as quickly as they enter into that very brief period of their existence. Help the young to enjoy being young, dear God. Keep them from having too many regrets from having passed through this challenging parenthesis in their life. Help them to make the most of these exciting moments so they can happily and anxiously move with joyous anticipation to those next challenging stages of living. Help them to move forward with such full-filled satisfaction that they will never have to say to themselves: "I sure wish I were young again!"

Single People

There are so many single people living alone these days, O Lord. Young people and old people and those single people in-between. Many of them sometimes feel so very alone, dear God. I know some of them want it that way but not all of them do. I have heard some of them talk about their one-sided conversations at their kitchen tables and the leftover food that would have been eaten if there had been someone else near at hand to eat it with them. I have heard some of them speak of their beds which have grown too big for them to sleep comfortably in anymore and their dwindling hopes for a life's bed companion growing smaller and smaller as each day moves on to the next one. God, it isn't just about food and tables and beds that single people talk about. It is about not having someone around to whisper wonderful things to anymore. Not having someone to love and to finish their spoken sentences with. Not hearing an echo to your own laughter. God, be close to single people. They need your presence in their lives.

Finish their sentences for them until they find someone else to do it with. Whisper in their ears how much you love them in case they never find anyone else to say those very same words in their presence. Be an echo for their joyousness so they don't drown in their own solitary laughter. These are very special people dear God. Those single people. Help them to understand that just because they are single people doesn't mean they have to be alone and content with life as it is for them, unless they simply want it to be that way.

Faking It

He was faking it, dear God. He acted so confident and self-assured. He appeared to be on top of everything but he wasn't really on top of anything at all and he knew it. In fact, most everyone else around him knew it too. It was painful watching his self-confident charade. The more unsure he felt within himself the more he seemed to bolster his outward appearances with boastful and prideful proclamations of certainty and assurance. The embarrassment that others around him felt for him was enormous but no one seemed to want to say a contrary word about his charade to him. Like the mythical king, this person was, indeed, very naked and everyone acted as if he was beautifully clothed. Truth had taken a holiday. Everyone was faking it. Social lying begat more social lying and everyone was taking part in it. It became more and more difficult for anyone there to stop and speak up for the truth. O God, please keep us from being prisoners of our fears and feelings of inadequacies. Clothe us with a clearer perception and respect for the truth about ourselves so that others won't have to be so embarrassed by our duplicities. Give us the courage we need to resist the temptation to fake who and what we are. Give us the tenderness and boldness we need to speak this truth gently and honestly to those people who feel unable to resist lying about who they really are or who they want to be. We know that covering up or faking it in life does not ever quite free us from the worst fears we have about ourselves. Give us the quiet assurance in knowing that the complete truth about ourself can actually set us free from the grip of many of the fears we have. Help us to trust and believe that being on top of some of the little things in life can eventually lead us to the feeling that we can come out on top of the bigger things as well. Help us to understand that telling the truth about our inner fears is the best weapon we have in chasing those terrible fears away. It would be so wonderful if all the emotionally naked people around us could be wearing clothes again so the rest of us wouldn't have to lie so much about them in order to spruce up their appearance.

Making Excuses In Life

He was filled with excuses, O God. Excuses he used to explain and to justify his underachievements in life. Over time these excuses had hardened into irrefutable reasons for his failures. Success seemed to be beyond his reach, he would say. And, of course, he had multiple reasons to explain why this was so. He had somehow convinced himself that the power to be successful in life came from the outside not from the inside of a person. It was clear to him that outside powers and forces were somehow opposing him. He was convinced he didn't have a chance at success because of these outside oppressive forces. The game of life, he felt, was stacked against him. O God, keep us from making excuses for ourselves. Protect us from the terrible danger where excuse-making can so easily evolve into rational reasons that limit our life's choices and chances. Help us to more clearly see that the liberating power within us is so much greater than any limiting power that could ever exist outside us. Help us to understand that life can be stacked any way we want it to be stacked. Help us to realize that we are the ones doing the stacking, not some unseen outside force. Help us to simply try to do our best in life. Help us to understand that doing one's best in life is what is actually meant by being a successful person in the first place.

I Love Passionate People

Dear God, I love passionate people. I love people who are so filled with desire and feelings that their energetic life force within them spills over its edges into the lives of all the rest of us who are privileged to be near them. I love it when the baseball batter stretches a double into a triple and slides into third base with his hat flying off his head and his arms and legs bent at angles that guarantee he will be sore in the morning. I love it when the music conductor's baton is bent with the emotion of a piece of thrilling music that only yields its latent beauty when the passion of the leader is equal to the passion of the composition itself. I love people who are passionate about their beliefs and whose spirit simply glows when they are given an opportunity to express their ideas openly. Fill me with this glorious passion, O Lord. Give me a passion for life. Give me a passion for others. Help me to be one of those people others wish to stand near to. Give my spirit a glow within it that will not be content until it finds a dark corner to transform and illuminate. I love passionate people, Lord. Fill me with your presence so I can be one.

In Between My First And Last Breath

Dear God, the first thing we do in life is to take a big, deep, breath of air into our lungs. Sometimes we do this so very quietly that no one hears our grand entrance. Often, however, our entrance to this life is a noisy affair accompanied by the irritated cries of an infant who feels as if he or she has been rudely awakened from a long nap before they were quite ready to be born to life. It sounds almost as if it is a protest cry of sorts. The very last thing we do in life is to give this vaunted breath back again to the one who gave it in the very beginning. Breathing in began it all in the beginning and breathing out gently ends it in the very end. In between, we are hardly conscious or aware of the profound rhythm of life we keep sustaining by taking this life-giving air into our lungs and then letting it out once again. Over and over we do this with scarcely a thought that what we began as a baby will someday have to be reversed later on. That what we received in infancy will have to be given back again later at some unspecified moment in time. Help me, O

God, to listen to my breathing. Help me to not only feel and hear its rhythm but its message to me as well. Help me to more fully understand that what gets filled up also, someday, has to be emptied. Help me to fill my very short time in between with loving and healing actions of compassion. Give me the deep satisfaction of knowing that when I give my last breath back that I used my breathing experiences in life to sustain and heal the ones you sent for me to care for along my way. I know, dear God, that I wasn't able to control the moment when my first breath was given to me nor will I be able to fully control my last one either when it is taken away but please help me, dear Lord, to wisely control what I do with it in between.

Losing And Finding a Job

She was a victim of downsizing, dear God. The company for which she had worked for many years had just let her go. Her performance was excellent. In fact, she was admired for the extraordinary human-relations skills she possessed. "No one can do the job like Mary," her co-workers would often say. But now she is gone, dear Lord. They didn't need Mary any longer. "Nothing personal," they said as she left on her last day of work. "It was a bottom-line matter of cutting our expenses," they explained more fully. However, it felt very very personal to Mary, O God. The fact that her leaving helped their bottom line expenses didn't help her personal feelings of failure, inadequacy, uncertainty, and fear that followed her out of the building on that day as she carried the small box of personal belongings away with her. Memories of all those congratulatory words of praise now seemed hollow to her. She was overcome with a profound sense of self-doubt. The little things she used to tackle with hardly a thought of their difficulty now have begun to loom as major obstacles for her. She has, subsequently, become frozen in a state of inaction. She wants to go forward with her life but her wounded self-esteem is keeping her immobilized in neutral. Please jump-start Mary, dear Lord. Help her to know how very special she still is. Help her to understand that nothing has changed in her. Help her to know that she is still that wonderfully gifted person she had always been. Help her to know that the real bottom line in life has nothing to do with a company's finances. Make her see that she is already a successful person, even if she doesn't have a job right now. Make her aware that being filled with your life-giving spirit is the true bottom line that any company which eventually hires her will be richer indeed for having hired her.

Have A Happy Birthday

She had a birthday, Lord, and we all sang to her. We applauded her too. All of us were very happy for her but she really hadn't done anything special to deserve the overwhelming attention we were all giving her. In thinking about it, dear God, birthdays aren't really about doing things at all. Birthdays aren't so much a reward for doing special things as much as they are a reward for just being there. Our happiness with this dear lady's birthday was simply our way of saying: "We are glad you are here in our presence because you are important to us. Important to us not just because of the many things you have done but because of who you are and because you still are. You are still among us this year and that gladdens our hearts." What a wonderful moment a birthday is, O God. It is that one single day in someone's life when we can all say to that person how glad we are that they were born and that they are still present among us to bless and enrich us with their life. It seems to me, O God, that the 'happy' in 'happy birthday' is really our way of expressing our happiness with them. I have a feeling that it is this happiness within us that puts the 'happy' in their birthday as well.

The Fastest Way To Get Rich

"A penny for your thoughts." she said to me as she noticed my pensive mood. The first thought that came to my mind, dear Lord, was that this lady really needed to update her cliches. She surely must have known that my thoughts were worth much more than a penny. There is simply nothing anyone can buy anymore for a penny. Certainly even the smallest and least significant of our thoughts must be worth a lot more than a mere penny. However, it quickly became clear to me that her statement wasn't about money at all. It was about intimacy. She wanted to share something with me. She wanted to give me her attention and interest in exchange for my giving her my thoughts. One for the other. An even trade. But when I finally gave in and shared with her my thoughts I realized that I hadn't really lost any of the thoughts I had given away to her at all. I still had them all. The only difference was that now we both had them. And when she gave her undivided attention and interest to me she really hadn't lost the interest she had in me at all. She still had it all even though she had given her interest in me away to me as well. What we both gave to the other we also kept for ourselves. We were both richer for what we had given away. Sharing is such a wonderful thing, O God. The more we do it the more we seem to have left over for ourselves to enjoy long after we have given some of it away to others. I think sharing must be the best bargain in the universe, dear Lord. In what other way can we be so enriched by what we have given away?

When Someone Is Too Good To Be True

I heard someone the other day, O Lord, refer to a certain man as being "too good to be true." In their mind they thought he was so good that he must have had some unattractive, hidden agenda people couldn't see. An angle. Some sinister self-seeking motive that was camouflaged by a decent, kind, and loving exterior. They seemed to think that no one that good could be for real. Where has all this cynicism come from, dear God? What have we done to create such suspicious perceptions of another's good character and good intentions? Why are we so inclined to think the worst of one another rather than the best? Help me, dear Lord, to gladly welcome goodness when I see it. Keep me from trying to minimize the goodness that I see around me by voicing hasty disclaimers or self-serving qualifications of the goodness that I see around me. It seems to me, Lord, that if there wasn't so much cynicism and suspicion in our world there would be a greater full-throated expression of joy for the genuine goodness that is clearly in full supply all around us. Help me to make more room in my heart for the good people I bump into each day. And, when someone says to me that they think someone is too good to be true, help me to be the first to suggest that the other person who is too good to be true is probably too good to be denied.

The Most Important Body Part

Dear Lord, almost all of my body parts still work. My feet carried me to this place of prayer today. My eyes helped guide my way here as well. My ears can still hear the ice-cream truck go by as I open this conversation with you this morning. I am really fortunate. Some of my best friends cannot walk, cannot hear, and cannot see. Other friends of mine have body parts that are breaking down or wearing out as well. But, fortunately, their minds still work. Our minds will sometimes take us back to another time and to another place and, for a moment, our minds can make us feel young again. Our minds can make us feel as if we could still climb that tall tree and still run that challenging race. And in that moment of joyous reverie, we reach out in our mind to grab the lowest limb of that quickly-remembered tree and all of a sudden we discover that our hands are much older than our mind. We are reminded, in a flash, that all of our body parts have, indeed, changed. They are still in the same place they have always been but they are not doing what we once could make them do. I am happy, dear Lord, that most of my parts still work but I know it will not always be this way. Keep my mind forever young, dear God, so that when I can no longer climb that remembered tree, my mind will still reach out and want to.

My Daughter Is Getting Married

My daughter is getting married, dear Lord. How could she be doing that? Didn't I just buy her a bicycle for her eleventh birthday? Didn't we just finish making the final payment for getting her teeth straightened? Where did all the time go, dear God? Are children becoming adults faster these days or are parents like me just slowing down in their ability to remember how fast someone can fall in love once they have straightened teeth? I like the young man she has chosen, dear Lord. This is not an easy thing for me to say, O God, seeing as this young man has recently removed me from the position of being the most important man in my daughter's life. I am sure I will get over it but it will probably take a couple of grandchildren that look a lot like me before I will be a fully happy father once again. All in all it is a wonderful thing for all of us that she is getting married. Her new husband will get an additional tax deduction and I'll get my old bathroom back again all to myself.

Improving Our Prayer Aim

I had a humorous thought as I got ready to pray to you this morning, dear Lord. In my mind I thought of a little child with her cheeks all filled with air and her lips all puckered ready to blow the candles out on her birthday cake. All of a sudden her puckered lips let loose with a mighty stream of air, blowing everywhere but missing all of the candles on her birthday cake at the same time. Over and over she tried until she finally blew all the candles out on her cake after many frustrating trial and error efforts to do so. I couldn't help but think, dear God, how our conversations with you are often a lot like that. Our conversations with you are quite often trial and error efforts. We open our mouths to pray and the words come rolling out in a torrent of hot air. Words come flying out in all directions but many of them do not quite hit the mark or clarify adequately what we feel we need to say in our prayer. We pray harder and harder, just like that little girl did with her puffed-up cheeks, thinking that if we increase our energy that it will somehow improve our aim. It never seems to work very well for us that way. It just seems to increase our frustration. Help me, dear God, to have a clearer picture of you in my mind so that I won't have to experience so many trials and so many errors when I want to talk to you. Help me to understand that if I could see and feel you more clearly and intimately in my heart that I could probably speak to you more comfortably with half the effort. Help me to improve my aim so I won't have to work so hard at throwing my inarticulate words and thoughts against the wall to see what sticks and what clearly does not.

On Being Invited To Dinner

Dear God, my wife and I were recently the invited guests for dinner at the home of two of our best friends. The food they prepared for us was wonderful but the atmosphere they created for us in their home was even better. The couple who had invited us to dinner had worked together all week to make that evening perfect for us. They were good at hosting such intimate and loving moments for their guests because they had been doing it together for many years. It was wonderful watching their generous love for one another transform our evening with them into a night of romantic enchantment. Words of praise and adoration bounced back and forth between the two of them as if they were playing tennis with their affection and love for one another. They were clearly not on their honeymoon but it certainly looked and felt as if they were. When we were ready to go home we felt filled both in body and in spirit. We left with a greater feeling of compassion and love than we had when we arrived. But I couldn't help but feel a little sad at the same time. I felt sad because there are some people whose invitations to dinner have not given us the same sense of fullness and joy we felt after dining with this enchanting couple the other night. We have said our goodbyes at the front doors of other homes we have been invited to, feeling the fullness of their meal but also feeling the emptiness of their spirit. Tonight was different, O God. We felt full all over.

Hearing Clearly What Is Spoken

Dear God, I thought I heard what she was saying but she informed me that she hadn't said what I thought I had heard. She felt she had spoken clearly but that I had not heard clearly. I apparently had heard what had not been spoken. Communication is a wonderful thing, dear Lord, when it works but it can be a terribly frustrating thing when it does not. I have to admit that sometimes when I am talking or listening to someone that it almost feels as if our words are like two ships passing in the night. Words passing from one person to another without touching the other person's understanding at all. There are times when I can understand the meaning of each single word a person speaks but when the words are all put together in a sentence their meaning quickly disappears or feels confusing to me. My problem, dear God, doesn't seem like a speaking problem to me at all. It seems more like a listening problem. Please help me, Lord, to listen better. Keep my mouth closed a little longer so my ears can listen a little more effectively. Help me to listen more accurately when a person is trying to say more than what he or she is actually speaking to me in words. Give me more successful experiences at listening so I am able to conclude my conversation with that person by hearing exactly what he or she was trying to say to me in the first place. Help me to listen as clearly as other people think they are speaking.

Making The Last Telephone Call

Dear God, if we had the time to make only one last telephone call in life before we died, I wonder who would be that person we would want to receive our final call? I wonder how much thought we would have to give before we dialed that final telephone number? I wonder what we would actually say to that other person when they answered the telephone? And, even more importantly, I wonder if the words we would speak to them in that final moment would ever have been spoken to them before we made that final call? Are our words, dear Lord, more valued when there is very little time left to hear or speak them? I would hate to be faced with the dreadful option of only being able to make one final call at my very end, O God. I would want to make many more calls than to just that final last one. I would also want to say final words to many people I deeply cared about that I had previously spoken to many times before. I wouldn't want any person I cared about to be surprised by any particular last sentiment I might reveal in my final telephone call to him or her. I would want my final words to simply excite a wonderful familiar reverie of other moments of joy and closeness we had shared with one another many times before. Keep my heart open to the people I meet daily, dear God. Help me to make many caring telephone calls to others while I still have the time to do so. I don't want anyone to ever feel slighted for not having received my very last phone call that I decided, in the end, to send to someone else.

Laughter Is The Best Medicine

Dear God, I wanted to share with you something very funny that happened to me this morning but I have second thoughts about actually doing that. You see, I can't help but wonder to myself whether my humor would be what you would be interested in giving your attention to this morning. I mean, after all, there are such weighty and serious matters of life and death around the world these days that must occupy the center of your heart's concern on a morning like this. Somehow it doesn't seem quite appropriate for me to be in a laughing mood in the face of all of these heavy concerns you must have on your mind. I really wanted, however, to have a good laugh with you this morning, dear Lord, but the thought of your serious agenda for the day quickly removed that smile from my face and the humorous twinkle at the corner of my eyes. Several hours have passed since I began this prayer with you this morning, O God, and it's afternoon now. I am in a much more serious mood. However, dear Lord, I have to tell you I don't feel any better for having put my humor on hold with you this morning. I personally feel you and I need more laughing times together. Humor, for me, really inflates the flat tires of my soul and it helps to soften for me those painful bumps I feel on the rough roads I travel each day. I really feel the need sometimes to pray to you with much more laughter in my voice. Help me to laugh a little more, with you, O God, so I will be better equipped to face the things in life that tend to make me want to cry.

Praying To God In A Time of War

Dear God, one of our nation's leaders said over the radio the other day: "God willing, we will be able to keep up the bombing of our enemy for the next three weeks." I wonder if the people on the receiving end of those bombs of ours were offering similar prayers to you, O God? Were they invoking your good will and support in their destructive designs on us as well? How do you answer such opposing prayers as these? I cannot help but wonder if it doesn't make you want to weep over the kind of invocations we offer to you by using your good name in doing so? How many games with prayerful words we often play to justify our hurtful moves on other people. We clothe ourselves with such pious expressions in order to cover the true nakedness of our bellicose intentions. Help us to understand, dear Lord, that wars are never made in heaven but, rather, they are aways constructed down here on earth where we live. Prevent us from getting heaven involved in what we, alone, have created on earth. Forgive us for the irrational decisions we have made by parting company with you in our going to war with others in the first place.

Leaving Well Enough Alone

Dear Lord, someone recently said to me: "Oh, just leave well enough alone." I wonder if that's not a big part of the problem we sometime experience when we try to forge close relationships with other people. Perhaps we are sometimes guilty of creating unrealistic expectations for closeness in our personal attachments with others. It seems that often we have difficulty in living with the plateaus that are sometimes created in our close connections with others. We sometimes have the feeling that if our close friendships or relationships aren't constantly getting better and better that something must be terribly wrong with them. In short, we have difficulty in leaving well enough alone. Help me to understand that sometimes even close friendships and connections in life need a leveling-off period for them to move forward in the future to a better place. It seems to me that friendships sometime need a time for consolidating the gains that have been achieved through previous shared moments with one another. Help me to see that these plateaus in human relationships are not necessarily a sign of failure at all but rather the staging grounds for even greater moments of joy and happiness that will come in the future. Help me to better understand that when things are going well enough between me and someone else that I don't have to do anything at all to improve them. Help me to understand that I can simply leave them alone and simply enjoy things just as they are.

Frightened To Death

She was so very frightened, dear Lord. The doctor said to her that more medical tests would have to be taken because he was concerned with the results of the preliminary tests that had already been performed on her. How quickly one's life can be changed by a simple blood test or x-ray, O God. How frightening life can sometimes become when disturbing news blocks our clear view of our future. Help my frightened friend to remember, dear God, that she has already lived a long life without ever having had a very clear view of her future. Help her to realize that it is a clear view of one's past that can also be as helpful to a person as a clear view of one's future. Assist her in recalling how helpful you have been to her in her past. Help her to understand that it is the past that is often the best predictor of one's future. Help her to realize that it was the faith which successfully worked in her past that can still work for her when her future is so very unclear for her today. Give her the quiet comfort in knowing that you are not just a God of history but that you are the God of the unseen present and future moments as well. Give her the conviction which realizes that it is not the seeing of things in life that makes us believe but that it is our believing that helps us to see things more clearly in life. Give her the assurance which realizes that it is not the facts that enable us to face our faith but that it is our faith that helps us face the unseen and sometimes scary facts of life.

True Greatness

I once knew a great person who was not a great scholar. I have also known many great scholars, O God, but not all of them have been great people. I have learned through observation that scholarship doesn't always lead to greatness and that many of the great human beings I have known have not arrived at their lofty position of greatness because of their scholarly accomplishments. It is a very rewarding experience, dear God, to set our feet on a path toward great learning and knowledge in life. Help us, however, to understand that it is not what or how much we know that makes us so great in the eyes of others as it is that special quality within us that makes others want to know us better. Help us to see more clearly that our greatness is not a matter of credentials on a wall as much as it is a spirit of kindness, tolerance, and compassion in our heart. O Lord, I think the world could well survive with less scholarship in it but I don't think it could exist for a single day without the spirit of good people who draw people's affection and admiration toward themselves like a magnet that is drawn to something metal. Help me to know as much as I can possibly know about the world I live in, O God, but help me first of all to be a person worth knowing in the first place.

Beautiful And Terrible Mornings

I woke up singing the other morning, Lord. It was a day filled with promise and anticipation. The words of an old hymn came to my mind: "Skies above were softer blue and earth around was sweeter green." It was simply one of those magnificent days. Blue skies and green surroundings. I was so glad to be alive. And in that moment of intoxicating jubilation the phone rang and the voice of an old friend gave me the sad news that a person we both knew and loved had taken his life. His life had become a life filled with overwhelming depression and pain and he had been looking for a way out of his pain. My friend told me that the person we both knew and loved had finally found that way. How differently life had spoken to our mutual friend this morning than it had spoken to me. How many miles away from his horrible pain I seemed to be in my intoxicating moment of happiness earlier this morning. Help me, dear Lord, to not be so caught up in my daily joy that I fail to see or feel someone else's daily pain. I know dear God that I cannot fill someone else's emptiness with my abundance but help me to at least be sensitive to the pain of those near at hand so that they might feel they are not standing alone in whatever personal misery they may be overwhelmed with in their present debilitating moment. When people around me are looking for a desperate door out of their anguish, O God, help me to be willing to step beyond my sunshine into their shadows to give them some comforting solace. Help me to find a way to show them the possibility, once again, of seeing skies that can be more blue for them and an earth that can be more green for them as well.

Putting Things Off

I hadn't seen my friend for a long time, dear Lord. One of the first things I said to him was: "How's your book coming along?" For several years he had said to me that he was planning on writing a book. "Well, I've not quite gotten started on the book yet but I am planning to begin writing it soon." was his reply. That had been the way he had responded to the same question I had been asking him for a long time, dear God. I think it is clear to me now that he is not going to write that book. His past failed efforts at writing his book is probably the best predictor that his book might just not come to pass for him. Our past can become a strong jail-keeper for us if we allow it to be, O God. We can become so easily chained and bound by our past decisions and responses to life. I am convinced that most of us do not want to become bound by those life-limiting responses we have made over and over again in our past. We want to be free to write that book or to climb that mountain. Help us to understand that our heart's future desires do not have to be limited by those good intentions we might have promised to keep in our past. Give us a sense of well-being and self-confidence that can break those endless cycles of our past failed attempts at life. Help my friend to understand that writing a book isn't going to make him a better person. Help him to realize that he already is a great person. I love my friend, dear Lord. I don't think I could ever love him more even if he eventually does write that book.

Surprised By Arrogance

O God, I am so surprised at how alive and well the arrogant spirit is these days. I see it in a children's sandbox where there always seems to be at least one little child who thinks he or she knows what is right or wrong for all the other little children in the box. I see that kind of arrogance revealed in the intimacy of some friendships or relationships where one, or sometimes both partners, seek to control the mind or behavior of the other. I am the most surprised, however, when I see arrogance flourishing in the hallowed halls of religious worship. It is there, in the inner sanctum of the sacred, where humility often seems to suffer its greatest abuse. I see so-called holy leaders sometimes pronounce with the greatest certainty their gospels of truth. And what is the most disconcerting to me is that they seldom waver or even hesitate in the boldness with which they speak on behalf of the Almighty. The one thing I have observed about arrogant people is that they are never tentative about anything. They often do not seriously or carefully ponder the complex matters that finite humans should consider when they contemplate the infinite mind of God and other similar transcendent matters. Arrogant people seem to make truth-seeking appear to be absurdly simple. One would think that such awesome or sublime thoughts would afflict them with a greater sense of humility but sadly, dear Lord, the arrogant seem to not be so afflicted. Keep me humble and open to your continual correction and guidance, O Lord. Empty me of my conceit so I can be more filled with your spirit. Keep me from being so full of what I think is right that I cannot see what you think is good.

Being In Charge Of our Feelings

"I'm sorry." she said, Lord. "That's just the way I feel. I can't help myself." That notion somehow just doesn't seem quite right or fair to me, dear God. It doesn't seem right for us to blame our emotions as if we have no responsibility at all for the feelings of hurt we unload on the people around us. I know there are those extra-ordinary moments in life when tragedy strikes us and we are overwhelmed by painful feelings which we cannot easily control. But it seems to me that most of the feelings we live with day after day, Lord, are there because we either don't want to take the steps to change them or because we have decided to nurse those awful feelings along so we can dump them on others around us when it is convenient for us to do so. Please keep me, dear God, from getting too much perverse pleasure from my negative and hurtful feelings. Keep me from playing the victim with my emotions as if they are in control of my life instead of the other way around. Keep me from bullying the people around me with my feelings and from suggesting to them that I really couldn't help myself when I actually could have. Give me the courage, Lord, to make the kind of decisions that will lead me to constructive actions that will spread joy all around me in the things I choose to do with my life. Be in charge of me, O God, and help me to see the wonderful ways I can also be in charge of how I feel and what I choose to do with those feelings.

A Laughing Matter

What she said to me, dear God, was that: "It was no laughing matter." I had a difficult time holding my laughter back because her situation seemed to me to be just that kind of situation. It seemed to be a laughing matter. Laughter seemed like the appropriate response I should have made in that moment when she spoke to me. I wonder how many arguments or how many wars might have been prevented in the past if both sides of some contentious exchange had decided to back off a little and laugh a big part of the entire episode away. I wonder how many broken friendships could have been prevented with a well-placed attempt at humor. I have seldom seen laughter injure or wound. More often than not, laughter seems to heal and revive broken spirits. There is a mighty trustworthiness in a robust belly laugh. I love those wonderful unguarded and unrestricted explosions of joyfulness when I witness them. Somber and overly-serious moments in life seldom invite the same spirit of warmth and closeness that humor does. Joyful laughter almost always comes to the rescue in moments like these. Laughter seems to me, dear God, to be the least class-conscious of all human emotions. A poor man who laughs joyously with all of his heart has a way of forcing even the richest person to smile and join in with a little of his or her own warmth and joy as well. The very same thing happens when a little child chuckles with glee and every grandparent who hears the child is forced to respond with their happy chorus as well. It should be a cautionary tale for all of us to realize that the one emotion that is almost totally missing in the mental illness section of every hospital is laughter. Help me to think of more reasons to laugh in life not more reasons not to. Help me to understand that many of the things I have to do each day should be seen as laughing matters. Keep me from being over-ruled by people who think they shouldn't be.

An Eager Learner

I saw something the other day that fully captured my attention, O God. I saw a learner. I saw a person who eagerly wanted to learn. He was different from most of the other classmates in the room. His classmates were sharing with one another what they felt they had already learned and they were content with that. But this student wanted eagerly to add more to what he had just learned. His classmates were contentedly filled to their capacity with the knowledge they had already received. He, however, wanted more. He had that hungry look in his eyes, dear God, that said he needed and wanted more than what he had already learned. That look in his eyes didn't change with the particular teacher he had or even with the particular subject he was studying. That look was always there even when his curriculum was altered. He was an eager learner. An eager learner for all kinds of things. Help me, O Lord, to be an eager learner too. Give me an eager, wide-eyed openness to the world around me. Keep me from being unduly influenced by either good or bad instruction. Help me to understand the fact that when I want to learn something badly enough then almost anyone will be able to teach me what I need or want to know. Dear God, help me to capture people's attention not by what I already know but by what I eagerly want to learn from them or even with them.

On Being A Failure

She said, "I feel like a failure!" I asked her, Lord, why she felt that way and she told me about her failed marriage and her limited capacity to earn enough money to support herself and her two small children. She told me how she got up every morning, dressed and fed her two children, took them to the baby sitter, worked all day at a not-too-satisfying job, returned at night to pick up her children, repeated her feeding and dressing ritual with them and finally prepared them for bedtime stories and prayers. After all of that, she worked even later into the night completing dozens of repetitive household tasks which never seemed to quite get completely finished. Each new day, she told me, was a carbon copy of the day before. Each new day reminded her of her failed life. Dear Lord, help us to refine our understanding of what it means to live a successful life. Help us to understand that one or two failures in life do not accurately define whether we have succeeded or not in life. Help us to know that simply showing up for work day after day when it would be so much easier to stay in bed under the covers is one of the signs of a truly successful person. Help us to see that it is the size of the unselfish heart not the size of the salary that separates failures from the successful people in life. Help this single mother to understand that people who are the true failures in life seldom worry about their failings. Help her to understand that sometimes very successful people will often live with the secret regrets of their own moral short-comings. This woman's life seemed like a real success story to me, Lord. She recognized the mistakes she had made in life but dauntingly refused to take the course of least resistance every day of her life. She showed up for work and she showed up for life. I think we really need more failures like her in this world, O God.

The Bed That Clarifies

I think, dear Lord, that it would be much better in some ways if we could live our lives backwards. It would be better, I think, if we could begin our lives with the expanded understanding that life often gives us at the very time we arrive at the very end of it. There is such a clarity at the end of life that is not there when we start in the beginning. On our dying bed we see so much more clearly the folly of spending a lifetime chasing after wealth, messaging our egos, and pursuing a thousand different material delights. Lying on that final pillowed plane we seem to possess a clearer vision of the truly important things in life: friendships that are intact; family members that are close at hand; and a love and appreciation for life that constantly has surprised and blessed us in a thousand ways. Our late-model cars in the driveway, the respectable street address posted on the front door of our house, and the titles of accomplishments next to our printed name all pale in comparison, O God, to the things that really matter when our eyes are focused on the bedroom ceiling for the last time. Help me, dear Lord, to have a clearer vision of my end-time so I can better appreciate the path my life will have to take to get me there.

The Bothersome Trail Behind

"I cannot help myself!" he said to me, dear Lord. "My parents were divorced when I was young and we were very poor. I suppose that explains why I am where I am today. I just cannot help myself." What a sad and limiting view of life this man possessed, O God. What a terrible feeling it must be for a person to feel imprisoned by one's past. Where did we ever discover such a notion, O Lord? We often make so many excuses for not taking responsibility for our present moments and decisions. How much easier, we sometimes think to ourselves, it is to blame someone or something else for what happened to us on our journey to where we are in this present moment of ours. I think if we take this lower road dictated by some previous road we have traveled is a limiting prescription that will continue to keep us from taking a much higher road in life when we actually could have. Help me, O God to understand that bad experiences are only bad if we choose to define them that way. Help me to remember that all my experiences in life are behind me and that is exactly where they should remain. Give me the joy of knowing that the most important part of my life's journey is right where I am now and that I, if I choose to, can be totally in charge of what I can do and where I can go on this future journey of mine. Help me, dear God, to look more carefully and excitedly at where I can be going and not so intently at where I have been.

Moving God or Moving Me?

"Where were you when I needed you, God?" Those were the words I heard her speak, dear Lord. "I trusted in the thought that you would be near at hand when I cried out to you for help. So, I cried out for you to help me and there was no answer. Not a word. There was no answer from you when I was looking for an answer." Her face was the face of the disillusioned. It was the face of someone who had lost her best friend or perhaps had lost someone she thought was her best friend. She had come to feel as if you, O God, had come to be more of a friend in name to her than a friend in deed. I heard her mumble to herself once again: "Where were you, God, when I cried out to you for words of counsel and I heard no voice? Where were you when people I know have plead for a helping hand from you and they received no helping hand?" I wanted to say to her, dear God, that you were right where you have always been. That you were holding the universe together keeping the balance of oxygen in the air just right so that she could breathe long enough to shout out those words of doubt and frustration at you. I wanted to say to her that you were keeping the Earth's temperature delicately controlled so that she wouldn't literally burn up before she expressed her cynicism and anger toward your so-called disinterested ways. I wanted to say to her that you were looking over her shoulders and weeping alongside her while witnessing the terrible circumstances of her life. I wanted to whisper to her that you are still standing nearby her side trusting in her intelligence, in her faith, and in the courage you have given her as weapons to deal with such terrifying moments as the ones she was currently dealing with. I wanted to tell her that you hadn't moved at all but, rather, that it was she who had moved. I wanted her to know that the best help she could ever experience when tough times come to her is for her to make the effort to move back closer to where you still are instead of complaining that you weren't trying to move closer to where she currently is. I am going to tell her this, O God, because I need to take some of my own advice. I think we both need to do a little moving.

Some People I Like and Dislike

Dear God, let me share with you some thoughts about the kind of people I like and don't like. I like people who are warm and friendly. I like people who act as if it is not necessary for them to be in my presence for them to value me. I like people who greet me when I walk into a room. I do not like people who treat me as if I am invisible and who give me the impression that I am not significant or necessary to their existence when I walk into a room. I like people who say "thank you" for the things they have received from me and from others. People who ignore this social grace give me the feeling that they see what has been given to them as an entitlement not as a gift. I like people who are interested in me. People like that make me profoundly interested in them. I do not like people who give me unwanted advice. They make me feel as if I am not acceptable or appreciated just as I am. I like people who do good things for others and then suffer amnesia so the rest of us don't have to suffer their wearisome re-telling of just how good they have been toward others.

I like people who will kneel on one knee to talk to an elderly person sitting in a chair or to a little child who walks into a room so neither of these two people will be forced to look up in order to have eye-to-eye contact with them. I like people who form negative judgments about other people slowly and if they do, they find a way to forgive them quickly. I do not like people who take the biggest piece of food on a plate so that others are left with only the very small pieces to enjoy. This helps to clarify for me those who are inclined to be selfish in their choices in life. I like people who like people more than principles because the one is real and the other is just an abstraction. I love it, dear God, when the new people I meet are just like so many of the wonderful people I already like. All of these wonderful people I like are the perfect lubricant for my soul which I require for what can sometimes turn out to be a very abrasive day for me.

Growing Older

Dear God, it is usually not considered a very smart thing to admit that we are getting older. We have creams, hair dye, and stretch pants to cover up all the many telltale evidences of our aging. The statement: "I'm getting old." is never a boast. It is always a complaint. We treat our aging with as much embarrassment as we did our teenage acne several decades earlier in our youth. The aging process itself surprises most of us with its amazing stealth and our denial of it is our first line of defense against it. But this denial is more and more difficult for us to maintain, dear Lord, especially when the stairways really do seem more steep than they once were and our memory really does seem less clear as to why we chose to climb those stairs in the first place. All I know, dear Lord, is that my medicine cabinet is now, for the very first time in my life, actually filled with medicine. Help me, dear God, to grow older with grace. Keep me from resenting the potions, the pills, and those pants with the stretch waistlines that are helping me to graciously live with that reality. Help me to understand that youth was a time we lived by our wits and that old age is a time when we can learn to live by our wisdom. Help me to find comfort in the fact that wit can be pleasantly replaced by wisdom and that it can be especially adaptable to the sunset years of our lives.

Compassion Or Justice?

Dear God, it has been my observation that compassionate people are canonized and people who are concerned with justice are crucified. We love the lover and we often despise the person who champions fair-play in life. I feel myself pulled between these two noble life choices in life, dear Lord. I have observed that it isn't very easy to be either loving or compassionate toward people who do not play fair in life. I admit it is anger that wells up within me, not compassion, when I am assaulted by these cruel expressions of injustice, O God. The more I focus on the world's injustices around me the less compassion I seem to feel toward some people. On the other hand, the more loving I try to be toward everyone around me, even toward the oppressor and the unjust, the more dim my concern for justice seems to become. A love for everyone has a way of sometimes blurring the lines between right and wrong and between justice and injustice. I am in a real quandary, O Lord. I don't know if I would rather be canonized or crucified. I would be thrilled to think that I could be both. I would be terribly embarrassed if I found out that I was neither.

Back-To-Back Religions

I spoke to someone the other day, Lord, whose religious background was greatly different from mine. He looked at life quite differently from the way I did. However, the more we talked to each other the closer we began to feel toward one another. It was almost as if we were standing back to back to one another but looking in opposite directions. It was clear that we were looking at life very differently but we felt so very close to one another while we were doing the talking and listening to each other. I couldn't help but think that perhaps it was not the specific direction toward which we were looking that was so important after all but, rather, that we were looking and exploring matters of great importance respectfully and trustingly together. Maybe looking seriously and reverently with someone at life's important concerns is ultimately as important as any actual agreement on the specific details of what we might be exploring together. All I know, dear God, is that I felt a kinship with this person as we explored the greater meaning and purpose of our lives. We didn't agree on all of the specifics we explored together but we felt incredibly and spiritually close to one another in our disagreement.

Humor

Someone said something very funny the other day, O Lord. All of us who heard the joke laughed uproariously. That is, all of us except one person. One person didn't understand what was so funny. He simply didn't get it. Humor can sometimes be a puzzling emotion, O God. It seems to me that humor is as much mental as it is emotional. Other emotions like fear, sadness, sorrow, shame and joy don't seem to require as much mental thought as does humor. In these instances we are merely confronted by situations that awaken these specific emotional responses and without taxing our minds at all we are immediately overwhelmed by these appropriate feelings. But, humor seems different somehow. Humor seems to require our minds to be aroused before our feelings can be similarly aroused. Why is that so, Lord? Why are our humorous responses in life so closely connected to our mental awareness of life itself? Is our ability to laugh at the world around us in some way a measure of our understanding of this world? I would very much like to be able to laugh more than I do. Help me to better understand the world around me so I won't feel so left out the next time everyone else in the room is laughing and I am not.

Things That Pleasure

Dear God, I was speaking to a mother the other day who told me she was driving her car and when she came to a stop-sign there was a homeless person standing at the side of the road. He had made a hand-made sign on which he had written the words: "Could you help me buy some food to eat?" The lady reached into her purse, rolled down her car window and gave the man some money. Her young daughter who was sitting in the back seat sucking her thumb, removed her thumb from her mouth and asked her mother: "Did you get a God-tickle from doing that?" The mother was astonished to hear her daughter frame her question in such an odd way. "Well, I guess I did" she said. "It pleased me very much to help him out and I hope it pleased God too that I did it." Dear Lord, please help me to get a God-tickle out of the things I do each day. I want the things that I do to bring real and lasting pleasure to me and I want it to please you as well. Many of the things I do for my own pleasure don't please me for very long and I am not sure they please you very much either. Give me your tickle, O God, and make it last for a longer time. I cannot help but think of what that little girl said with such innocence. Her innocence speaks to my own self-centeredness. Tickle me with the pleasure that this mother discovered when she reached beyond herself to fill someone else's genuine need.

Our Valentine Greetings

It dawned on me, dear Lord, that we have holidays honoring famous people; holidays honoring our mothers and fathers; holidays honoring religious people who have profoundly shaped our lives for good; and we even have a holiday to honor fools. However, it dawns on me that we also have one holiday to honor a human emotion. We have one special day all year to honor the emotion of love and to celebrate those who have experienced this love in their own lives. It seems right that if we have a holiday to honor the fool we should certainly have a holiday whose focus is love. I am convinced that it is that quality of love that has created the reason for the existence of many of the other holidays on our calendar. It was the Native American's love for the new settlers in our country which gave birth to our Thanksgiving Day. It was the patriot's love for our country which created our celebration of President's Day. Our parents' love for us children made us want to set aside a special day for us to honor both our father and our mother. Love seems to be the very basis of so much of what we honor and celebrate all year long. I have a feeling, O God, that every holiday greeting card we send this year to someone else is really a Valentine's greeting card in disguise.

Healing Affection

It is so wonderful to observe a room filled with affectionate people. It is a deeply moving experience to see people freely embracing one another with warmth and friendship. In these tender moments of affection, O Lord, the cares of a difficult week or the burden of a painful encounter are momentarily set aside. The crushing feelings of our personal failures or disappointments are quickly mended by another person's warm embrace extended freely without judgment or recrimination. There is nothing else in the world, O God, that brings me back to life so quickly as a friend's healing touch of affectionate love and acceptance. It is that touch which extinguishes my desire to fight or to engage in some sort of flight to escape the pain. The warm embrace of a friend is the most gentle of all attractions that helps me to resist the urge for revenge or retaliation. It is like an announcement to the entire world that my war or hostility with others is over. That all is well and that tranquility has returned to me and is flourishing well within my soul.

Thank you, dear God, for touching and embracing me. Help me to be one of those in a room filled with people who is willing to move someone else's heart to gladness by my friendly embrace so that everything will be all right again in their world.

My Grandchildren

I love my grandchildren very much, dear Lord. I am so glad I didn't have my grandchildren before I had my children. I think having my children first was a great preparation for having my grandchildren later on. I used up most of my inexperience, anxieties, and frustrations on my children years ago so my grandchildren today have a much more relaxed grandfather than the father my children had when they were growing up. I remember how much pushing and pulling I did with my own children, Lord. I don't do that at all with my grandchildren. Just watching them and simply enjoying them was and is so much more pleasant than pushing them around. I love the secrets my grandchildren have shared with me, especially those secrets they tell me about their parents. I can't help but wonder if my children told my parents secrets about me. I love it when the grandchildren come to visit. I love it when they leave as well because one of the best parts of being a grandparent is being able to love those wonderful little reproductions of oneself without having to be totally responsible, hour by hour, for them. I certainly am glad I had children, because I couldn't have had such wonderful grandchildren without them.

Infinite Understanding

Dear God, I feel that when I talk to you and try with all my heart to understand your divine and infinite spirit, that it is a little like trying to divide the number three into the number four. I can do it of course, but when I do I find there is always a little something left over after I have performed that mathematical task. I feel that way about you too, O God. No matter how much I try to understand you and your holy ways, there is always something left over which I am not able to fully understand, explain, or clarify. Help me, dear Lord, to be more content with what I already know and understand about you. Help me to be satisfied with knowing that I will never quite know it all. Help me to be at peace within myself in knowing that what I already understand of your divine spirit will not be altered significantly by my knowing more about you. Give me the humility to be content with the part of you I already cherish. Forgive the arrogance in me that thinks I can define or explain fully who you are. Please keep me from being a know-it-all in this matter. Help me to understand that my greatest joy in life will probably not come from an increased knowledge of what I do not know about you but that it will come, instead, from an increased appreciation of the good and blessed things I already know quite well.

Ignorance And Arrogance

I was so upset with a man's ignorance the other day, dear God. I found myself trying very hard to be charitable toward him but his arrogant insistence that he was completely right about so many things quickly eroded my natural inclination toward tolerance and forbearance. His overbearing arrogance even seemed to magnify his ignorance in my eyes. He prided himself in having all of the right answers for most everything. He was a man, O God, completely devoid of humility. His vaulted position of pride turned him into a bullying presence in every conversation he held. It was a sad and intimidating experience to observe him in action, dear lord. He could not see what was so painfully clear to the other thoughtful people in the room. He could not see his own severe lack of understanding about so many things. With terrible blindness on his part, he tried to overwhelm his environment with prideful boastfulness. What a pitiful sight he was to see, behaving the way he did. But it was not his ignorance that bothered me as much as it was the fact that he was dressed up in the garb of such a superior attitude that troubled me the most. Please keep my spirit humble and teachable, dear God. I don't ever want to look in a mirror and see the face of that man looking back at me.

Talking But Not Listening

I sat in a room the other day, dear Lord, with a person who would not stop talking about himself. He told one story after another about his many experiences in life. It wasn't as though those stories were boring stories at all. The truth is, they were all quite interesting stories, but they were all stories about himself. He somehow must have felt, O God, that I needed to hear everything about his wonderful life. He scarcely took a breath at the end of each story before he started a new one. He didn't so much talk to me or with me as much as he talked at me. I felt as if I was just the excuse he had been looking for to talk about himself. He never once asked me to make a comment on what he had said. He never asked me a question. And he certainly never asked me if I had any interesting stories of my own to tell. I felt reduced to a thing. I felt like an object. I felt sad and disappointed because at the time he began his conversation with me, I felt like a person.

Religion And Politics

O Lord, someone said to me the other day that religion and politics shouldn't mix with each other. I couldn't help but wonder to myself: "Why not?" Everything else seemed to mix with politics. Money certainly mixes with it. Show business and big business easily mix with it. Even immorality of various kinds mixes happily with politics. It seems to me, dear God, that if there ever was a time when national politics needed a good mixture of sincere piety in it that now would be a good time for such a mixture to take place. I cannot help but think, dear Lord, what a difference a sincere religious spirit would make in political life. "Good God!" would no longer be just an expression of a politician's frustration with a political adversary. It could be his or her recognition of the importance of some transcendent truth. "Jesus Christ!" might not be just an epithet sworn in anger but, rather, a simple acknowledgment of one of history's most respected and revered spiritual persons. And, "Thank Heaven!" could be more than just the releasing of emotional tension between two politicians but, instead, an acknowledgment on our part that sometimes we all have to reach higher than ourselves for transcendent relief, insight, and inspiration. It is probably true, O God, that religion and politics aren't mixing very well these days, so please help us to find better ways where we can make that happen. Help us to understand that if we who claim to be religious fail to find a good way to influence our politics then the darker forces in life certainly will.

Crying Is Good Medicine Too

I am sometimes surprised, dear Lord, at the many different circumstances in life that have caused me to cry. When I have missed someone a great deal in the past I have found it very difficult to hold my tears back. When someone I love has died I have cried even more. When I have disappointed myself or someone I love and respect because of some careless or thoughtless behavior on my part, I have not been able to keep my tears from flowing. When I am touched by someone else's failure in life and then witness their humble contrition for the wrong they have done to another, I find myself often crying with them and for them. And, sometimes, when I am overwhelmed with happiness and joy at how wonderful life can be, my eyes begin to well up in tears and before long my entire face is wet with jubilant pleasure. I have not always been able to cry so easily, dear Lord, but there is one thing I have discovered as I have grown older is that I feel so much better since I have learned how to do it. I am sometimes embarrassed when these lubricating moments come to me, O God, but I am always so much more relieved when they do. I have heard that laughter is the best medicine. Perhaps that is true but I have also learned that crying is sometimes just as healing. I have discovered there are times when laughter is seriously out of place. I have yet to find many places where crying is.

The Spoken Word

The spoken word is so very powerful, dear God. Words are like a window into our soul. They reveal so much about the kind of people we are. Those harsh and critical words I sometimes hear people speak make me wonder if that person is very unhappy or unfulfilled within. Kind and complimentary words, on the other hand, I think are spoken by people who have a deep and personal contentment within themselves. Words are certainly wonderful mirrors or reflectors, dear Lord. We see so much of a person's character revealed in the word choices they make. And, sometimes when no words are spoken at all, when words should be spoken, that is just as revealing as well. The inability or unwillingness to speak a word of kindness or encouragement when such a spoken word is called for is a profoundly disturbing thing to behold. I cannot help but wonder, dear God, whether a person who doesn't speak up when he or she should speak up is actually alive inside. Isn't death the time when no more words are spoken? Please protect me, O God, from speaking words that injure. But, also protect me from the deathly silence that comes from speaking no word at all when a kind and caring word is what is called for in that moment.

Tolerance And Intolerance

Dear God, some of the best people I know are intolerant people. They have a difficult time tolerating laziness, unkindness, any task left only partially completed, and a host of other things in life that have mediocrity written all over them. I love this kind of intolerance, O God. I love the passion for the truth, for the beautiful, and for the good that these so-called intolerant people possess. Should any of us ever be forced to tolerate lies, ugly and repugnant behavior, or the evil intentions that people sometimes throw in our faces? Isn't our intolerance of such behavior an acceptable response to those deep convictions within us that should not be compromised or diluted? Dear God, help me to be passionate about the life-affirming ideas that enflame my soul. Help me to speak my heart and my mind with undiluted conviction. However, when others feel differently than I do about important matters, help me to behave toward them with a kind and tolerant spirit. Guide me in extending to them the same kind of freedom to speak the truth as they have come to see it for themself. Let my words be words of unwavering conviction but make my attitude toward others to be one of charitable tolerance and respect.

Enthusiasm

She was so enthusiastic, Lord!. Every word she spoke was super-charged with heart-pulsating energy. What she was trying to say was so much more than the actual words she chose to clarify her thoughts. It was her feelings and her emotions that riveted those words of hers to my mind. It was as if her whole being was enflamed with the transcendent importance of what she was sharing with those of us who were enthralled with her speaking. How could I not listen and take in her every word? I was taken captive by her unbridled enthusiasm. I could hardly breathe for fear I would miss something in the very act of taking my next breath. Her entire spirit was saying to me: "This is very important! Don't you dare miss listening to any part of this!" Give me that kind of enthusiasm, dear God. Fill me with your spirit and burn within me the importance of what I have to share with others. Give my words the added weight that comes from a soul that is on fire. Let me speak words of importance with such passion that people will fear to take their next breath.

Angry Again?

He was angry, dear God. His friend had made him so very angry. But the anger wasn't his friend's fault. It was his fault. The anger was his anger. The anger belonged to him and to no one else. The simple truth was: his friend had not made him angry at all. The anger was his own choice. He had made himself angry. There were other choices he could have made but this man made the choice to be angry. The moment had been too much for him. It was a matter of self-control. He seemed to lack the skills and the humility to master the moment and so the anger-moment always seemed to control and master him instead. His easy escalation into anger revealed a weakness in his character almost as if blinding neon lights were flashing on and off, saying: "I am frightened and I feel powerless and I am as mad as I can be about this!" There is such a nakedness about anger, dear Lord. It reveals so much about ourselves that we want to keep hidden. It unmasks both the controlling arrogance of our domineering spirit and the hidden weakness of our character. Please help me, O God, to be more humble about the person I am and less demanding about what I think I deserve in life. Build in me a quiet restraint so I will not rush headfirst with my anger over people I have no right to control.

Blessed Receiving

Dear God, I have often heard the remark that: "It is more blessed to give than to receive." I don't disagree with that at all. This world would certainly be a more blessed place if there were less takers and more givers in it. I love to be around people who are generous and giving. I don't like being around the opposite kind. But I wonder, O God, if sometimes it is more blessed to be a receiver than it is to be a giver? I know a lot of people who are not very good receivers. When they are offered a compliment or a gift or simply some other expression of love or appreciation from someone's grateful heart, they find some way to deflect or refuse the gift. These people are often wonderful and giving people themselves but they don't often realize how hurtful to the giver their inability to be a gracious receiver can be. I have sometimes noticed, dear God, that the need for someone to give a gift to another is sometimes greater than another person's need to receive it. Help me to be aware of that. Please don't let my reluctance to receive stand in the way of someone else's need to express their love and gratitude for me. Help me to understand that sometimes it really is "more blessed to receive than to give."

Supporting Falling Skies

People are very anxious to talk to you, dear God, when they feel their sky is falling down upon them. I don't blame them at all. I think falling skies are a pretty good time for all of us to look for big-time divine help. I know you are a God of the good times and the joyful times but I also know you make house calls when terrible emergencies arise as well. I am so very glad you do this because I think that this is one of those times when we need you to come to our nation's house. It is in such frightening moments as the ones our country is now facing that we realize how weak and inadequate we sometimes are to handle the difficult and terrifying experiences which have come our way. Under most conditions we manage to muddle through and make the very best of our difficult moments but what we are dealing with right now feels very different, Lord. We are facing great challenges to our faith and our ability to persevere in the face of considerable evil. A lot of things seem to be falling down on us right now, even a little bit of our sky. We need your help. We have treasured the stories of how you have helped desperate people in other desperate moments in times past. We know you have not been limited at all by those different brackets of time other people have lived in. We know you are the God of all time. Not just the God of some time. Comfort us, O God. Help us to know that you can hold up both the skies that threaten to fall down upon us and to protect those of us who are busy running for cover at the same time. Help us to find comfort in the knowledge that no evil force around us can ever bring down what you choose to hold up.

Three Little Words

I heard a song the other day, dear Lord, that spoke about the importance of three little words. Those three words were: "I love you!" I couldn't help but think that there are many other three-little-word phrases that are also important. A few of those came immediately to my mind: "Please forgive me." "You go first." "You are important." "Haste makes waste." "I am sorry." "Practice makes perfect." "I was wrong." "Let me help." And, of course, "Hope springs eternal." I am sure there are many more, O God, but I couldn't help but realize how often good advice comes wrapped in such small packages. Help me to remember these little phrases which mean so much to all of us when they are spoken at just the right moment. Help me to understand that it isn't how much we say to someone else that is as important as what, specifically, we choose to say to them. Help me to more fully comprehend that good speeches are not measured by their length but rather by their depth and their sincerity. Help me to be a person of fewer words, O Lord, but let these words be carefully chosen to bring great comfort and encouragement to those who are waiting and wanting to hear them.

The Harmony Of Words And Heart

She said all the right words to me, O God, but what she said with her unkind spirit wounded and hurt me. No one could ever have faulted her for what she literally spoke to me in words but what she actually communicated to me with her unkind politically-correct speech inflicted considerable pain on me. Her words made her look very good but her spirit made me feel terrible. O Lord, how ugly beautiful speech can sometimes be when it camouflages a venomous heart. Please make my healing words harmonize with my healing heart. Prevent me from saying one thing with my lips and something very different with my spirit. Make me as kind and loving on the inside as I try to appear to be on the outside. I love beautiful words, dear God, but a beautiful heart is equally as lovely. Keep me from ever having to choose between the two. Bind my words and my heart together so tightly that when I open my mouth to talk, my heart will speak the same language.

The Best Sentence

I was constructing a sentence of response in my mind while she was speaking her next sentence to me. I didn't even hear that last sentence of hers, dear Lord, because I was listening too closely to my own unformed one I was framing in my mind. I realized that I wasn't really having a conversation with her at all. I was only having a conversation with me. What she was trying to say to me didn't seem nearly as important to me as what I was thinking about saying to her. My talk with her was like bouncing a ball off of a wall. All she was to me in that moment was a wall. She was just someone to bounce some sentences off with. My sentences, of course. She was just a wall, not anything more important than that. I feel very badly, dear God, with how I had used her. She may have had some very valuable things to say to me that day. Some important things, perhaps, that I needed to hear. But I will never know that because I didn't hear a word she said. I only heard the words I was speaking to her in my mind. Please help me, O God, to keep my ears more open than my mouth. Help me to become a better listener. Help me to better understand that sometimes the very best sentence in the world is not the one I am in the midst of constructing but, rather, the one that is coming to me from someone else who desperately needs my attention. Slow down my speech and speed up my hearing. Let me take my turn at being the wall.

Shame And Guilt

"I'm nothing but a failure!" That's what she said to me, Lord. "All these years of living and I am nothing but a failed life," were her exact words. She was completely overcome with shame, that awful feeling of not having lived up to other peoples' expectations of oneself. Guilt was there too, the awful feeling that she had not lived up to her own expectations for herself either. Her shame and guilt finally issued their verdict of her unworthiness. She stood condemned by them with nothing good she could say for herself. It was as if someone had hung the scarlet letter 'F' for 'Failure' around her neck. It was clear to her that everyone must see her in the very same way she had come to see herself: a failure. O God, please protect me against the destructive power of both shame and guilt. Keep me from being overly unkind to myself and give me the strength to withstand other peoples' excessive and unkind judgements of my life as well. Help me to try as hard as I can in all that I do and help me to be content with having given my best along my way. Keep me from being overly critical of my failures. Help me to realize that there is no special virtue in being an unrelenting perfectionist. Help me to develop a thicker skin when I encounter other perfectionists who make unrealistic demands on my performance. Help me to entertain shame and guilt in very small doses in my life because I really do want some sunshine left for me while I continue undertaking my life's journey.

Interest At First Sight

Dear Lord, I heard someone reply when he was asked how he had met his love-partner in life. He was asked: "Was it love at first sight for you?" His response was: "No, it was interest at first sight." How insightful these words are, O God. It seems true to me that in most cases interest almost always precedes love. In fact, love can hardly flourish between two people without considerable interest from both of the parties having existed first. Perhaps that is why loving relationships sometimes come to an end between people who had once been lovers. They come to an end not because they have suddenly lost their love for the other but, perhaps more importantly, they come to an end because the two people have simply lost interest in one another. One's interest in the other person almost always seems to disappear first and then the disappearance of their love for one another seems to follow soon after. Maybe the very thing that good loving relationships need more than anything else is not more love but more genuine interest in the other. Help me, O Lord, to show more abiding interest in people I am deeply fond of so my loving relationships with them can continue to blossom and grow. Keep me from becoming too quickly disinterested in those love connections I value. Help me to understand that love is not an accident at all but, rather, the delightful result of our purposeful and continuing interest in another. Help me to become more aware of the explosive possibilities that genuine interest in another can produce between people. Remind me how my unselfish interest and concern for another can lead to the loving creation of a longed-for soulmate. Help me to also understand how disinterest can also quickly make orphans of almost everyone we meet.

At The End

For most of us, dear God, the least-welcomed guest of all in life is death. We postpone death's visit to us in numerous veiled ways. We sometimes chase after life with a reckless abandon and hope the presence of death will never ever find us or make itself known to us. It isn't until our hair turns white and our hearing is taken from us that we steal a look over our shoulders and realize, with a sudden chilling clarity, that we are losing the race in outdistancing the grimmest of all reapers. In that moment of clarity the truth speaks the same message to the mighty and to the humble alike: death wins. It always has the last word. Help me, O God, to see my end more clearly and peaceably while I am still somewhere in the middle of my life's journey. I certainly do not want some abrupt or sudden disclosure of this inevitable truth revealed to me at my very end. Help me to understand that a serene ending to life is always tied to a serene connection to those wonderful middle passages of one's life. Help me to trust that my leave-taking from this familiar world is not really an end to me at all but rather only a new beginning for me. Thank you for being with me when I started along my way many years ago and for constantly checking in on me during those middle steps of mine as well. I am at peace with the notion that death has the last word in my life but I am also comforted by the fact that I have complete control of so many other words I can utter as I move on through my life. So, I choose to shout these powerful words of mine to all who will listen to them in the universe where I live: "To Life!!!"

Thanks For the Memories

I opened my dresser drawer the other day, dear Lord, and there it was. It had been there for over 30 years. It was a little baby's stocking that one of my children sent me in the mail telling me that I was going to be a grandpa. All the old feelings of pride and happiness flooded my heart again just as they had over 30 years earlier when I first received this little package in the mail. How priceless keepsakes are, dear God. They condense and store so much of who we were and how we felt, once upon a time. And when we hold these priceless treasures in our hands again for the second time, they not only restore those once-in-a-lifetime moments for us again but they also restore some of those youthful feelings for us as well. We immediately feel so much younger and more energized. We feel transported in time and space and we more clearly understand how truly wonderful recovered and remembered moments of joy are. We discover that time doesn't diminish these blessed moments but, rather, it enhances them. Thank you, O Lord, for the memory of so many treasured experiences in my life. If I must lose something as I grow older, please let it be my eyesight or my hearing or even my health but let me keep my memories intact because there are so many wonderful things packed comfortably inside them. I will never tire of remembering them all, again and again and again.

Fragrant Blessings

Smell the flowers. That's what I think of, Lord, when I feel myself out of breath from running too fast from here to there. Flowers are what I need to smell when I lose my perspective about what's really important in life. Smelling freshly mowed grass or hay is what makes me think of my happy childhood days on the farm. The smell of a little baby's powdered body after its bath is the perfect remedy for me when my stress levels have risen above my comfort zone. The clean smell of the fallen rain reminds me of the promise of a fresh new beginning of life. It says to me that no matter how soiled my personal situation ever gets, I can start afresh with others I may have wounded or harmed. Thank you for giving me a nose, O God. So many of my best blessings are just a sniff or two away. Help me to be a glorious fragrance wherever I go so the scent of my arrival will be a pleasurable experience for all others to experience as well.

Down Time

I am feeling kind of down today, Lord. I don't know why. I just feel down. No one has crossed my path in a harmful way at all today. I don't feel any sense of personal failure crushing against my heart and soul. There is no disappointment that has left me in a wanting condition. I'm just down and I don't quite know why. Please be down with me, O God. Keep me from being alone in my down time. Lead some needful person to my path. Help me to be a part of someone else's down-moment so I can get my mind off of my own. I find considerable comfort in remembering what I have heard many people say to me before: "This too shall pass."

Fixing People

Dear God, help me to get past the seductive temptation of trying to fix the so-called broken people in my life. There are so many broken people around me, O Lord. More often than not I find myself unable to resist the impulse within me to try to fix or rearrange those broken things in their lives to make them feel better. This arrogance on my part isn't very flattering. Help me to understand that the best fixing usually comes from the inside of people themselves not from his or her outside. Keep me from imposing my will and my views on others. Cultivate a deeper trusting spirit in me to take people just as they are without trying to make them over in my own image. Help me to listen more and to talk less. Help me to appreciate more quickly and to criticize more slowly. Help me to fix people by loving them rather than by rearranging them. After all, I really do want a few friends around me at my life's end.

Cynicism and Sarcasm

He was so cynical and sarcastic, Lord. I was sorry he had come into my day. It was as if a dark cloud covered and extinguished the sunshine I had brought into that moment. I have noticed, O God, that cynicism and sarcasm always seem to travel together. Cynicism sees nothing but closed doors in life and sarcasm is the cynic's typical irreverent response to everything. I am so weary of such people. The cynic's lost faith and hope provides nothing to enrich the space he or she occupies in life. The person intoxicated with sarcasm finds nothing at all worthy of his respect or reverence as he moves through time and space. Every thing or every person around this kind of person is quickly and efficiently dismantled or trashed by a sarcastic person's flippant and cutting analysis. Cynicism and sarcasm fill nothing and they empty everything. Please, dear God, fill me with more than enough of your sunshine to neutralize the clouded presence of these two unwanted visitors in my life. Please don't let them take my sunshine away.

The Time Of Our life

Dear God, I just had a birthday the other day. I have more birthdays behind me now than I will ever have ahead of me. For me, O Lord, birthdays are not as much a reminder of how much time has passed for me as they are an estimate of how much time I have left. With more time behind me than ahead of me, I am reminded of what a precious commodity time really is. Time didn't seem as precious to me when my hair was dark and thick. In fact, I scarcely gave any serious attention to it in those days. In those youthful days I had used up very little of my life's allotment of time and I thought that, along with such things as my energy and my ambition, these things would never be in short supply. So, I frivolously wasted much of my energy and carelessly spent a great deal of my time without realizing that these were very limited and precious resources that someday would be gone forever. I have a much clearer view of things today, O God. I am joyfully looking forward to those years ahead that will be mine. They will not be wasted. They will be cherished. I know I have less time left to enjoy than I once had but I have a greater capacity with which to enjoy the time I do have. Scarce resources are always the most valued. People who possess scarce resources are the ones most blessed. My recent birthday has placed me in the enviable company of the most blessed. What a great birthday present I have just been given!

Won't-Power

My friend told me the other day that he lacked will-power, Lord. He told me that he kept repeating over and over again the very things he knew he shouldn't be doing. He felt he knew the answer to his self-defeating behavior that left him feeling like a failure and a fraud as a human being. "It is my lack of will-power," he said to me. "I simply lack the will-power to resist my terrible temptations." Dear God, I don't think my friend lacks will-power at all. I think he lacks won't-power. I have seen him in action and he seems to have plenty of will-power. He does exactly what he wants to do. Whatever he wills to do he finds plenty of power to do it. His will and desires are plenty strong. It doesn't seem to me that he needs more will-power at all. I think he needs less of it. I think he needs a little more won't-power. I think I need less will-power too, dear Lord. Temper my will, O God. Give me a healthy dose of won't-power so that the next time I confront my private demons I will be able to say to myself: "I won't give in to this!" Help me to develop an I-won't-give-in kind of spirit when I am tempted to do what I know I should not be doing. When my demons speak to me help my I-won't-give-in desires to come forth more quickly than the I-will-give-in ones. Help me to feel that wonderful power that comes when we learn to say: "I won't do this, because I know it is not good for me." Help me to learn how every good decision I make in life empowers me to follow up by making another good decision later on. Will-power and won't-power. What powerful forces they have been in my life. I wish I had learned much sooner how well within my grasp both of these powers have been available to me all along.

From Something To Everything

Dear God, a person who had made a lot of money in his lifetime once said to me: "Be careful, money isn't everything." He went on to say: "Come to think of it, money is hardly anything at all." He was trying to tell me that money, all by itself, will not make a person happy in life. But if that is true, dear Lord, why do so many people work so hard to obtain it? Why do people, when they are given the choice between a job that pays very well and another job that pays far less, almost always choose the higher-paying job? Why was this wealthy man's message not reaching and convincing more of us of his truth? There have been a lot of wealthy people who have been sending this very same warning to us for a very long time. Why is it that this repeated warning keeps falling on such deaf ears? Why are some of us so intent on trying to prove that these rich people are not telling us the whole truth? Is it that we think we are the sole exceptions to this rule? Are we convinced that we are those few rare individuals who could be rich and wonderfully happy at the same time? Help us to learn from other people's sad experiences, O God. Help us to acknowledge that not many people have ever said that love and generosity and kindness and tolerance aren't everything. Maybe the reason that no one has ever said this is because they, indeed, **are** everything.

Depressed And Sleepy

He is so depressed, Lord. My friend wants to spend all of his time in bed. His depression, I think, is really just a cover for the tremendous feeling that he has failed at everything he has tried to do in life. All of the joy has gone out of his life. He is feeling as if he is just the shell that is left over from his former self. He feels that the slightest pressure of life might crush and break him so he is hiding from life by sleeping. He can barely move from day to day because of the horrible weight of this numbing sadness of his. It keeps him anchored in bed with no will or desire to move on. My friend is in a terrible place, O God. Please free him from his self-defeating sleep. Help him to see that he is so much more than what he thinks he has done or not done in life. Temper his tendency toward exaggerated self-criticism. Cultivate in him a more forgiving attitude toward himself so he can find a way out of his bed and a way out of his sadness and a way back into the happiness he once enjoyed.

The Art Of Renunciation

Dear Lord, I am trying to learn the art of self-renunciation. I mean, I am trying to think less of what is so important to me and me only and more of what is important to others as well. I so often feel like a little boy who is reaching through the narrow bars of a cage to remove a beautiful toy inside only to find that he cannot remove the toy because his closed fist around the toy cannot slip back through the bars. My exaggerated wants and wishes are like that closed fist that continues to rob and keep me from the peace and contentment I need and want most in life. Help me, O God, with two things. First, help me to know exactly what things I should renounce in favor of the other more important things in my life. Keep me from holding on to those less important things which have little lasting value for my soul but which continue to seduce me with their transient charms. And secondly, Lord, once I have a clear picture of what I should release in my life, give me a clear picture of those things of value I should attach myself to. Once I have learned to live on less, help me to learn to live with what is abundantly more. Help me to learn how less can become more for me and then help me to have the enthusiasm and desire to embrace it.

Both Half Full And Half Empty

Dear God, I heard someone the other day pose a question before a group of us leaders who were meeting together. She said to us: "Do you usually think of the glass of life as being half full or half empty?" Of course I had heard that question posed many times in my lifetime and, depending on how I was feeling at the moment, I would usually answer either "half-full" or "half-empty." I have come to realize upon more careful reflection that the question, as we usually hear it, is not very well phrased. The question, as we usually hear it, calls for a clear choice between two opposite perceptions of life. The question forces us to align ourselves on the side of either being optimistic and upbeat or being pessimistic and discouraged about life. The simple truth is, O Lord, most of us feel both ways about life much of the time. I am sometimes quite up and optimistic about some things and at other times quite discouraged and even pessimistic about other things. It seems to me that our challenge, Lord, is to not let either perception of life overwhelm or influence our good sense and our will to continue living courageously regardless of how up or down we may happen to feel at any specific moment in time. Keep me from being discouraged, O God, when my life does not always have the balance I would like for it to have. Give me the comfort of knowing that I can continue to feel your stabilizing presence within me whether my glass seems half full or half empty at any given moment or even when I cannot find my glass at all.

Hearing What I Didn't Say

Thank you, dear Lord, for listening to me! So few people do anymore. Thank you for hearing what I didn't say. What I couldn't quite find adequate words for. What I was afraid to openly say. Most people don't hear that well. I mean, they don't hear people's unspoken words very well. What they hear are the things that are clearly said. However, so many people don't hear the thoughts and feelings that were meant but were left un-said. You, O God, hear those things and I am so very glad you do. Sometimes my tongue is so tied to my feelings of self-consciousness that I have a hard time putting my important thoughts into clearly expressed words. Sometimes I wonder if there are even the right words for some of my thoughts. And when I finally discover the right words I find that sometimes I lack the courage I need to speak them. Help me to be a better listener, Lord, so people will have the courage to reveal to me what they want and need to reveal. Help me to hear what people want to say even when they cannot find the right words to say. Help me to finish people's sentences for them by listening a little better to what they are trying real hard to get across to me.

Faith - A Decision

"Where do you get all of your faith?" That is the question she asked me, Lord. She admitted to me that she had no formalized religious faith. She said she often had little faith in the people she could see and that she had no faith at all in a God she could not see. I told her that I thought the way she responded to people and to God were related to each other. I suggested to her that being open to having faith in a God we cannot see actually helps us to have more faith in the people we can see. I confessed to her that our experiences with the people we can see affects how willing and how well we can trust or not trust a God we cannot see. I tried to explain to her that faith almost always works in both of these directions, not just in one. I also tried to explain to her that having faith is a decision we make ahead of time not a conclusion we reach after all the facts are in. I said to her that faith is what we decide in the morning to begin the day with not what we end up with at the end of the day when all the evidence has been gathered. I don't know if any of my suggestions made any sense to her, dear Lord. I had the distinct feeling that her real problem was not in having or not having faith at all. I felt her real problem was her lack of courage to make a faith-decision ahead of time that would call her into a life of humility and surrender to others whom it appeared she had given up on a long time ago. It seemed to me that she needed to make a decision that would help her surrender the cynicism that had poisoned and distorted her attitude toward so many important things in her life. A decision to let go of her arrogance and feelings of superiority that kept her disconnected from the life-giving richness that others could provide for her life. A decision to live as if you, God, were indeed real and then to be willing to wait for that reality to bear fruit in her life.

Living With Our Differences

Dear Lord, I have read that the astronauts who move around in their spacecraft are the best of friends. It has been revealed that they worked closely together for many months in preparation for their venture into space. They spent hundreds of days and hours huddled together in a space much smaller than the size of most of our living rooms. As united as they were in their exciting celestial objective, one cannot imagine a more diverse group of human beings anywhere. Their differences in race, gender, nationality, and even religion, O God, seems not to have diminished their ability to bond with one another or to complete the tasks a grateful nation entrusts to their care. These very real differences, which often impede our performance of even the most simple tasks on earth, seemed not to have been insurmountable burdens to these astronauts in their performing complex tasks in the heavens. Does their exalted orbit around the earth give them a clearer perspective from which to view each other, dear God? Does their viewing points significantly affect their viewpoints? If so, then put me in orbit too, dear Lord. Give me a more exalted perspective from which I can take a fresh look at myself and the people who share my space with me. Help me to look at the people who are near at hand and help me to see no insurmountable differences between us. Help me to just see people. People with whom I can labor to accomplish noble purposes. O God, these astronauts seem to make life work the way it is supposed to work and they have succeeded in doing so in a very small, cramped space. Help me to make the best use of the space you have given me and help me to fully appreciate the people you send to share this confined space with me as well.

Contented Eyes

I saw the man's bicycle leaning against the building, Lord. His bicycle had a very small trailer carefully bolted to the rear axle. Inside the trailer, tightly tied together, were: a small tent, a sleeping bag, and a tiny canvas sack for food and other personal items. Strapped to the handlebars of the bicycle was a little portable radio loudly playing cheerful music that captured the attention of the people walking by the man's mobile home. "Everything I own in life is on that bicycle" I heard him say to a woman who had stopped to talk to him. The bicycle man was nicely dressed and the contented look in his eyes truly surprised me as I strained to listen in on the private sidewalk cordiality these two strangers were extending to each other. The man with the bicycle did not have much stuff, O God, but he had very contented eyes. I have so much more than he had but I have to admit that all too often my eyes are not nearly as contented as his were. I had the strange feeling, dear Lord, that this man could have lost his bicycle and even his radio and his eyes would have remained the same. I want those kind of eyes, dear God. I want the kind of contentment that isn't tied to my ambitious accumulations in life. Help me to have a clearer understanding of just how much I really need in life in order to be happy. Help me to know when enough is enough and even when enough is too much. Give me a deeply contented heart so that my eyes won't change when the treasured things I have gathered around me are either lost or taken away.

www.ingramcontent.com/pod-product-compliance
Lightning Source LLC
Chambersburg PA
CBHW031404290426
44110CB00011B/254